Jesus Compared

BOOKS BY THE AUTHOR

Jesus Compared

A Study of Jesus and Other Great
Founders of Religions

by

CHARLES S. BRADEN, Ph. D.

Professor Emeritus
History and Literature of Religions
Northwestern University

Englewood Cliffs, N. J.

Prentice-Hall, Inc.

1957

PRINTED IN THE UNITED STATES OF AMERICA

50943

To
"Dutch"

Preface

―――――[□]―――――

"HOW DOES JESUS COMPARE WITH CONFUCIUS, OR BUDDHA, or Mohammed?" As an historian of religions, I had been asked this many times. Might it not be a proper subject for a book? I began to search the libraries to see what had been written on the subject. Here and there I found a fairly detailed comparison of Jesus with one founder or another. There have been occasional Master's theses making comparisons of some aspect of Jesus' teaching with that of another; for example, the ethics of Jesus and those of Confucius. Numerous incidental comparisons have appeared at one point or another in books and articles. But I looked in vain for any systematic confrontation of Jesus with the other great founders of religions. Here, apparently, was a gap to be filled, and thirty years or more of steeping myself in the history and literature of the great religions had prepared me to undertake the task.

In preparing each chapter, I followed fairly consistently the plan of looking first at the sources of our knowledge of the figures involved, comparing the relative historical character of the material. I then noted the points of similarity between the individuals under comparison, discussed the differences between them, and finally attempted to set forth the ways in which their earlier and later followers came to think of them.

I had in mind as I worked not the specialist in the field

of religion, but the intelligent layman who might like to have some basis for evaluating the respective figures. The specialist will, I hope, find that I have made fair and adequate use of the work of the best scholars in the field.

Most of the chapters have been submitted to colleagues in special fields, and I am grateful for their suggestions and corrections. I am, of course, responsible for what finally appears in the book.

As an individual, I stand squarely within the framework of the Christian faith, of which, indeed, I am an ordained minister. Yet I have tried to be scrupulously fair in dealing with each of the figures I have compared with Jesus, setting forth as impartially as possible the pertinent facts in each case, leaving to my readers such value judgments as may properly be made. I dare not suppose that I have kept out all Christian bias from the treatment of these great personalities. I can only say that I have tried. It has always seemed to me that the Christian faith may safely be trusted to stand up alongside any others without any attempt on my part to misrepresent or to belittle them.

Serving as preacher at the College Church one Sunday, I chose to speak simply on Jesus. Many who heard the sermon insisted that it ought to be included in the book. This I have done, recognizing that it lacks the objectivity that I have sought to achieve in the remaining chapters. Perhaps I may be allowed to say that in all my study of the world religions across the years, and in the special research done for this book, I have discovered nothing that has in any sense lessened my deep personal loyalty to Jesus, whom I hold to be my Master, the one in whom I find supremely revealed the God of Christian faith.

Scripps College   CHARLES S. BRADEN
Claremont, California

Acknowledgments

———————————□———————————

WHO COULD WRITE ON A SUBJECT COVERING SO WIDE A RANGE OF time and varying cultures as this book does without deeply indebting himself to a host of previous workers in the field? To all these, the unknown as well as the known, the writer desires to express his gratitude. But some must be mentioned especially. To all copyright owners who have given permission to quote from their publications, I am very grateful. They are: George Allen & Unwin, Ltd; The Buddhist Society; Columbia University Press; The Clarendon Press; Doubleday & Company, Inc.; E. P. Dutton & Co., Inc.; Harper and Brothers; Harvard University Press; Alfred A. Knopf, Inc.; Lutterworth Press; The Macmillan Company; Macmillan & Co., Ltd.; John Murray; Oxford University Press; The Popular Press; Mrs. J. B. Pratt; Princeton University Press; Charles E. Tuttle Company; The University of Chicago Press; Yale University Press. Specific acknowledgment is made in appropriate footnotes throughout the volume.

My very warm thanks to Dr. George Cameron of the University of Michigan; Dean Earl Cranston and Professor Floyd Ross of the University of Southern California School of Religion; Dr. Clinton Loehlin, long-time resident of Amritsar, India, and student of the Sikh religion; and Dr. William A. Irwin, Professor Emeritus of the University of Chicago and Perkins School of Theology, Dallas, Texas, for reading various chapters of the book and making helpful corrections and suggestions.

Great also is my indebtedness to my good friends and colleagues at Northwestern University, Dr. Edmund Perry, my successor; Prof. Paul A. Schilpp, Professor of Philosophy; and Dean James M. McLeod, who graciously extended the invitation to deliver the John C. Shaffer lectures, which form a part of this book, and who showed me so many courtesies during the period of their presentation. To them hearty thanks.

CHARLES S. BRADEN

Table of Contents

———□———

1

Jesus

———————◻———————

STRIPPED OF THE LOVELY STORIES OF HIS ANNUNCIATION
and birth, the singing by the angels of "Peace on earth,
good will to men," the coming of the Magi, the flight into
Egypt, His presentation in the temple—all of which many
regard as literally true and others as only the tribute of love
and honor embroidered upon the simple facts concerning
the birth and childhood of a very unusual individual—
somewhere about four or six B. C. there was born into the
world in an obscure, out-of-the-way province of the
Roman Empire, a child who changed the very face of the
history of the world. Men of the West and, increasingly,
men of the East also, count time from the date of His birth.
At the very least, He must have been an extraordinary
person.

There is very little that we know concerning His childhood and youth. Only once do the canonical gospels—
our principal source of knowledge concerning Him—pull
aside the curtain to let us see a young lad of twelve, talking
earnestly with the elders in the temple to which His parents had taken Him on their annual pilgrimage. We don't
know what He said. He is only reported as reproaching
His parents mildly, asking, "Know ye not that I must be

about my father's business?" Then the curtain falls back again into place.

The Apocryphal gospels tell of deeds of wonder wrought by the growing Jesus, and later writers have sought to fill up the gap by the play of imagination upon them. Such an attempt is that of John Oxenham in *The Hidden Years*.[1] Another book that was sent to me recently purports to give, on the basis of revelation, a very detailed account of what Jesus did in every one of the Hidden Years. People of other faiths have had Him take long journeys into India or Tibet, where He was supposed to have learned the secret doctrines which He later imparted to the people. A fairly late guess puts Him in a monastery of the Essenes, a group upon whom additional light has been thrown by the recent discovery of the Dead Sea Scrolls. But, really, no one knows if He did aught other than share the labor of Joseph the carpenter and, after the death of the latter, take over the support of his mother and his brothers and sisters.

Suddenly, as it appears in the Gospels, He comes out of obscurity and seeks out a preacher who had begun to create quite a stir, attracting crowds to his ministry down along the Jordan river. John the Baptist he was called, because he baptized his followers in the river. Jesus sought baptism at his hands, although John at first demurred, recognizing in Jesus one the latchet of whose shoes he was not worthy to unloose. Was this a sudden flash of insight, or had John already known of this young Nazarene by reputation, who now came to him for baptism? The answer to this question, as to many another which arises concerning these early years, may never be known.

[1] New York: Longmans, Green and Co., 1930.

At any rate, to Jesus the experience was a crucial one. He felt an urgent necessity to get away and think it through. So He went away into the wilderness to be alone, to straighten it all out in His mind, and ultimately to determine the course He should thenceforth follow. This was no shadow boxing match through which He went, as the tempter again and again assaulted him. In the traditional three temptations, one can see the travail of soul that He must have undergone. Should he accept the spectacular, easy way—cast Himself down from a pinnacle of the temple, trusting that, as Satan promised, He would be borne up by angels lest He dash His foot against a stone? The novelist Costain in *The Silver Chalice* has painted a vivid picture of Simon the Magician boldly having such a tower built from which he would leap one day, upheld by cleverly hidden wires so that he would seem to soar above the people without falling, and thus convince them of his superhuman powers. And Hollywood gave it spectacular visible form on the screen.

Shall He win all the kingdoms of the world by bowing down to Satan and worshipping him? Shall He use His miraculous powers in His own behalf—turn stones into bread? What a lot of bread He could have made from the super-rocky hillsides of Judea, and how people would have flocked to Him for the loaves, had He chosen this course. Interpret as we may the three temptations, they were in the highest degree real—a normal occurrence after the baptism experience. In the end, He came out of the wilderness and embarked upon one of the oddest ministries the world has ever known. Where will you find its equal?

It consisted of going up and down the countryside, now in Judea, now in Galilee, now in Perea and the Decapolis.

Mostly, it seems to have been in the fields or by the side of the sea of Galilee, now and again in Jerusalem—only once outside the narrow limits of His own country, when He went into the region of Tyre and Sidon. Mostly, also, it was among simple folk who seemed drawn to Him—and to women and children. Of the latter He seemed to be very fond, though He never married and had children of His own. He is said to have taken them in His arms and blest them. Once, when the grown-ups would have sent the children away that they might not bother Him, Jesus rebuked them, saying, "Forbid them not, for of such is the Kingdom of Heaven," and on another occasion He said to His followers: "Except ye become as little children, ye shall in no wise enter into the Kingdom of Heaven."

It was about this Kingdom of God, or Kingdom of Heaven, that Jesus spoke most frequently. It seemed to be the very heart of His message. "Repent ye," He cried, "for the Kingdom of God is at hand." He tried to make it meaningful for simple folk by telling them, not so much what it was, as what it was like. And in so doing He used the language of the people to whom He spoke, making use of familiar images of the things of everyday experience to make them see His meaning.

To some women Jesus explained that the kingdom was like leaven, or yeast, which a woman took and hid in three measures of meal. Nothing here about the "event in history," the "kerygma," the "parousia," "the word breaking through," nor even about the "incarnation." They wouldn't have known what He was talking about. Sometimes I think that if the world must be saved through such obscure theological language, most of it is likely to be lost. These women knew what yeast did, even if they didn't know what caused it to do so. It leavened the whole lump. It grew, it expanded endlessly. That was the way of the kingdom. It was not static. He expressed the same idea of growth to some farmers by telling them that it was like a grain of mustard seed—the smallest of all seed—but, when grown to full size, the plant offered a place where the birds might come and rest and feed. Clearly this Kingdom was alive. There was in it a principle of growth and development.

And it was something of tremendous value. Changing the figure as he talked to His women listeners, Jesus said that it was like a woman who lost a precious coin. She just couldn't find it anywhere. You know how you feel when you have lost something. "Why, I had it only a moment ago. Where could it be?" It is so frustrating. "Now, let's see. I saw it right here. I had it in my hand, until"—and so we go searching, searching everywhere. The woman of the story did a thorough job. She swept the whole house, looked behind every piece of furniture and in every corner—and finally she found it. What joy! She was so thrilled and happy that she called in her neighbors and had a celebration right then. "Come," she cried, "rejoice with me, for that which was lost is found." And there was great rejoicing. Jesus said that the Kingdom of God is like that, precious beyond words.

He got the same idea over to a pearl merchant by telling him that the Kingdom of God was like a merchant in search of fine pearls, who, on finding one pearl of exceptional value, went and sold everything that he had and bought it. "It is the Pearl of Great Price, this Kingdom of God," Jesus said. To another, it was like a treasure found hidden in a field. Carefully concealing it, the discoverer went and sold everything else he had in order to possess himself of the land containing this great treasure.

It is interesting to see how Jesus varied His illustrations to suit His hearers. To fishermen, He likened the Kingdom to a net cast into the sea which brings up fish of all sorts, good and bad, to be sorted out—the good to be kept, the bad thrown away. To farmers, He said that it was like a field in which both wheat and tares had been planted. Together they must grow until the harvest, when the inevitable separation of grain and tares must occur. To shepherds, He spoke of the separation of the sheep and the goats, the one kind to go into the Kingdom, the other rejected.

In making it plain to farmers, Jesus told of the sower who went forth to sow, scattering the seed this way and that as he strode across the field. Some seed fell along the path, where the earth was beaten down hard, and the birds came quickly and gobbled it up. Some fell on rocky ground. Here the seed sprang up quickly; but, having no depth of soil, the plants were quickly scorched by the hot midday sun. Some fell among thorns, and the thorns grew more rapidly and choked them, and they produced nothing. But happily, much seed fell on good ground and brought forth, some thirty, some sixty, and some an hundredfold.

What matchless stories, so simply told that they could be easily understood and as easily remembered! This fact is one reason why I am inclined to believe that much of what Jesus taught, though handed down by word of mouth for a generation or two before being written down in the form we have it today, has come down to us substantially as He gave it. Add to this the fact that most of His sayings are concise, seldom lengthy, save in John, and often epigrammatic, as in the Beatitudes, and you have added reason to believe that what has been preserved is a substantially accurate report of His words.

Jesus' teachings were popular. People gathered about Him wherever He went. Sometimes He had to slip away from the crowds into the wilderness to get any rest or time for private, quiet prayer and communion with God. Once a great crowd, said to be some 5,000 people, followed Him into the desert, having apparently neglected to take any food along with them. When they were hungry and the disciples would have sent them away, Jesus had compassion on the multitude and fed them. Some say that it was by getting a small boy who had brought five small loaves and two fishes to offer to share it with the others. At the sight of this generosity, others brought out food which they had with them and offered it also, and there proved to be enough and more for everybody, so that a considerable remnant remained over. To some, explaining it thus seems to detract from Jesus—and, as a miracle worker, perhaps it does. To others, this is precisely the way Jesus worked His miracles—miracles of love and generosity, by getting people to share with their fellows.

He consorted with all sorts of people, even publicans and sinners. When complaint was made as to the latter, He said, "But the whole have no need for a physician. I am come to seek and to save that which was lost." It was the lost sheep, not those safely in the fold, which chiefly interested Him. The inimitable story of the son who asked his father for his part of the estate and went off to spend it in riotous living illustrates this. When the boy had run out of funds and his fair-weather friends had deserted him, he was forced to take employment at the hateful task of feeding hogs—he, a Jew, who abhorred these unclean animals. He came to himself and, reflecting on the plenty which even the hired servants of his father back home enjoyed, resolved to go back and throw himself on his father's mercy and beg for a job which would at least give him enough to eat. He would say to his father, "I have sinned against heaven and in thy sight; pray make me as one of thy hired servants." He started home.

Meanwhile, the father was away out down the road waiting hopefully for him to come home, and when he saw him, he ran and fell on his neck and kissed him and cried, "Bring hither a robe and put it on him, and let a feast be prepared, for this my son which was lost is found." And there was great rejoicing, for, said Jesus, there is greater joy over one sinner who repenteth, than over many who are righteous.

But with all its simplicity and directness, there was something about Jesus' teaching which troubled many people, especially around the towns and cities, where there were lawyers, and priests, and officials. This was His attitude toward the past, toward tradition, even toward the sacred law. Nothing was more sacred to the scribes and the Pharisees than the law, the sacred Torah. Any threat to it was not to be tolerated. Such a person as Jesus appeared to be was "subversive," and you know how people—I mean the "good, solid, sound" citizens—look upon subversives.

He was standing, at this point, directly in the tradition of the great prophets of Israel. There were always two traditions in Israel: the priestly and the prophetic. The priests were in general conservatives, who looked upon change as dangerous. The prophets were not bound in tradition. They were critical of their heritage, and were not afraid of innovation, believing that there was yet more truth to be known than had as yet been revealed.

Jesus had dared to say, on various occasions, "You have heard it said of old time, so and so, but I say unto you. . ." This was rank heresy. "Who did He think He was? A carpenter of Nazareth! And what good could come out of Nazareth? What right did He have to be setting Himself over against Moses and the Torah?" Clearly, something must be done about this. They began to put their heads together and to plan His liquidation, if I may use a term much used in our day.

The things He was saying! "My dear, have you heard what that Nazarene carpenter said?" I can imagine the tongues wagging. 'Blessed are the meek, for they shall inherit the earth.' That's a queer note. The man must be crazy." Indeed, that seems to have been the conclusion of the members of His own family, for on one occasion they went, His mother and His brothers—to Capernaum, where He was teaching, to take Him home. They said that He was *beside Himself*, which means "crazy, insane."

And weren't they about right? For He said such things as: "You have heard it said of old, 'Thou shalt love thy neighbor and hate thine enemy,' but I say unto you, 'love your enemies, pray for those who persecute you'." Everybody knew that was wrong. The way to deal with enemies was to hate them, to injure them, even to destroy them. Surely He didn't mean what He said.

And then one day He came out with this, as though the general principle were not enough. "You have heard it said, 'an eye for an eye, and a tooth for a tooth,' but I say unto you if anyone strikes you on the one cheek, turn to him the other also. If anyone would sue you and take your coat, let him have your cloak as well. And if anyone forces you to go with him one mile, go with him two miles." The hated image of a Roman soldier forcing one of them to carry his burden for a mile rose in His listeners' minds. Probably some of those who heard Him had been impressed into such service—and the bitter memory of the experience still rankled within them. How "balmy" could a man be and still remain at large? All very well to tell people to behave like that, but they'd like to see someone land one on His jaw and just see what would happen.

He seemed to possess unusual powers of healing, and the sick thronged around Him so that He could hardly move about. They even lowered a man from the roof of a house into the courtyard where He was teaching so that he might be healed. A woman with an incurable issue of blood pressed into the crowd just to be able to touch the hem of His garment, and was restored to health. So many demands for healing were made upon Him that He had little time to teach the people about His precious Kingdom of Heaven. He tried sometimes to get His little band of followers away from the crowd into a quiet place where He could pass on to them His inmost thought.

One day Jesus left Bethany, where he had been staying, and started into Jerusalem. The crowds gathered and hailed Him with cries of "Hosanna," spread down palm branches, and threw flowers into His pathway, as He rode a donkey into the old city. They even tried to make Him king that day, but He refused. He found the temple where He went up to worship overrun with vendors selling sacrificial animals and doves and grain, as well as money changers. The noise and clamor of these in the holy temple made Him indignant. He cried, "You have made my father's house a den of thieves and robbers," and, seizing a whipcord, He brandished it about, driving the sheep and cattle out of the temple. These overturned the tables of the merchants and the money changers in their haste to get away, and pandemonium reigned.

Now it became crystal-clear that Jesus was a dangerous revolutionary. What might Rome do if it learned of this disturbance? Roman officers had been known to deal very harshly with those who disturbed the peace. Machinery was set in motion to get rid of Him. One of His dissatisfied followers was bribed to deliver Him to the authorities on the first possible occasion. He chose to do it on the evening when they had celebrated the passover meal together in an upper room.

They had eaten together the last supper. Jesus had girded Himself and washed the disciples' feet. Then they sang a hymn and went out to pray in an olive garden now known as Gethsemane. Jesus knew what was coming. He had seen it as inevitable. He had been warned not to go up to Jerusalem, but, open-eyed to the danger, He had set His face steadfastly toward Jerusalem, and now could see clearly the end. He needed to be alone. So into the dark garden He went, leaving His disciples to watch below. He knelt at a great rock and prayed that He might meet this trial. His flesh shrank from it. He wanted to live. More than once He prayed, "Father, if it be Thy will, let this cup pass from me." It is related that in His anguish He sweat, as it were, great drops of blood. And in the end He was able to say, "Nevertheless, not my will, but Thine be done." Then He arose and came out of the garden, to be met by the betrayer's kiss and delivered into the hands of the soldiers.

Peter impulsively seized a sword and cut off the ear of the high priest's servant. But he was rebuked by Jesus, who cried, "Peter, put up thy sword. They who take the sword shall perish by the sword." Maybe after all He really did believe the things He had been saying. Here was a clear refusal to use force to defend Himself from what He most certainly knew would lead to His own death.

At the various trials, Jesus gave further evidence of His faith. Falsely accused, He made no attempt at defense. Did He remember the suffering servant of Isaiah 53, who "was oppressed and afflicted, yet opened not his mouth. Like a lamb led to the slaughter, and like a sheep before its shearers is dumb, so opened he not his mouth?"

When He was turned over to the soldiers to be scourged, they went about it with right good will. They said He was King of the Jews, and they dressed Him for the part. They put a purple robe on Him, gave Him a reed for a scepter, and pressed down upon His brow a crown of thorns. They struck Him. They kicked Him. They spat upon Him. But He made no effort to strike back. Nor did He rail upon them as did the thieves between whom He was crucified a little later. Hanging upon the cross, for a moment His human nature tore from Him an agonized cry, "My God, my God, why hast Thou forsaken me?" But as the blood oozed from His wounded side and His life ebbed away, He looked down upon those who were watching Him die—some soldiers, some civilians—and prayed, "Father, forgive them, for they know not what they do." His eyes dimmed. He hung for a while as though in a coma, then summoning the last of his fast-waning strength, He murmured in a low voice, "Father, into Thy hands I commend my spirit," and was gone.

Did an earthquake rock the city? Was the veil of the temple rent in twain? Did the dead come forth from their tombs, as the Matthew narrative says? And was it this which caused a hard-boiled Roman centurion who stood by to say in awed tones, "Truly this was the son of God"? Or was it this Galilean Teacher's superb acceptance of death upon a shameful cross at the hands of His enemies with a loving prayer upon His lips for their forgiveness as He died? Was it the triumph of what Channing Pollock called "The Terrible Meek"?

The story is ended. Or, is it? They took Him down before the beginning of the Sabbath and laid Him in the tomb of Joseph of Arimathea. They rolled a great stone against the door of it and sealed within it their hope. For the light had gone out of the world for the little group that had surrounded Him. A little later, two of them were walking along the road toward Emmaus, when a third joined them and asked why they were so sad. "O sir, have you not heard? We hoped that it had been He who would redeem Israel." They came to an inn. They sat down together to eat. As He broke the bread, their eyes were opened and they recognized Him. And He vanished out of their sight.

Two of the women who had followed Jesus went early to the tomb to annoint His body. And, lo, it was empty! Reports kept coming in of persons who had seen Him. He was not dead, then! The violence of the cross had not been able to destroy Him! He was alive, then—in the world still!

Paul, writing years later, was to assert that just as Jesus had appeared to the disciples, so also to him, "as to one born out of due season," Jesus had shown Himself. Confirmed in this faith by a powerful experience at Pentecost, this once discouraged, beaten group of disciples went out to win a world to Him, and for Him.

The centuries have come and gone. Men have differed enormously in their thought concerning Jesus and their attitudes toward Him. Some have called Him God. Some have called Him man. Some have called Him God-man. They have theologized and theorized about Him in every imaginable way; but, whatever the Christological level at which men have placed Him, they have agreed that in Him is to be found the clue to the nature of God and His purposes for the world. They have generally accepted as true His statement to Philip, who said to Him one day, "Show us the Father, and it sufficeth." Jesus replied: "Have you been so long with me and yet have not known me? He that hath seen me hath seen the Father."

And they have believed generally and still believe that whatever salvation means to man and his world is bound up in some way with Jesus. If it must come, as some believe, through a supreme act of God, it is nevertheless through Jesus as mediator that man attains to it, in this world or in a life hereafter. If it must come through man's own striving, in co-operation with God, it is still Jesus who, by His own life of obedience and sacrifice, and by His teaching, who shows the way. Many there be who in this modern day find it difficult to hold some of the older beliefs of a supernatural order. Yet large numbers even of these are perfectly convinced that only as men, individually and as a society, make His ways their own, is there any chance for that peace and security for which men individually and collectively so deeply yearn.

Understanding them, each in his own way, men the world over have come to believe the words spoken long ago of Him: "And you shall call his name Jesus, for he shall save His people from their sins."

2

Jesus and Buddha

---□---

IN POINT OF TIME, BUDDHA ANTEDATES JESUS BY SOME-
thing over five centuries, having been born near the
middle of the sixth century B.C. Both are Orientals, indeed, all the founders of the great religions were born east
of Suez. Jesus was born in Palestine; Buddha, in India—the
mother of four world religions. Both Jesus and Buddha are
now known and followed chiefly by people of racial or
national groups other than their own and outside the land
that gave them birth. Both started movements intensely
missionary in character which carried their respective faiths
into the distant regions of the earth and which are still extending their ideas and spirit throughout the modern world.
Both gave rise to movements that have had an enormous
influence on the cultures of many people, their literature,
their art, their philosophy, and their way of life.

Concerning the actual facts with respect to their birth,
their childhood, and their youth, little is known. Outside
of the literatures of the two faiths, there is almost nothing
in the way of information about them. Indeed, I have been
able to find no extra-Buddhist source material concerning
Buddha, and that concerning Jesus is extremely limited
and quite general rather than specific.

This does not mean that there is no dependable source material. The fact that such material is Christian or Buddhist does not necessarily discredit it. What is more natural than for those who most esteem a figure to be most careful to preserve knowledge of him? The difficulty is that eager devotion tends with the passage of time to embroider the facts with an overcovering of legend and story, so that it becomes difficult to separate out what is fact and what is legend.

The piling up of legend is very good evidence, indeed, of a core of fact which underlies legend. The possibility of gratuitously constructing a life of a Buddha or a Jesus upon no basis of fact is, it seems to me, very slight. Whence the impulse to such legend-making? To me, I must confess, it is much more easily reasonable to assume an historic basis for the legends than not, especially where, as in the case of Jesus, there is good substantial evidence that the stories about Him were in circulation within a generation or less of the time when He is thought to have lived. Legends do not take form so rapidly unless there is some historic basis upon which they rest.

Both figures, then, are known chiefly through the sacred literatures that grew out of their movements, and, alongside the canonical literature, there is a considerable amount of what may be called apocryphal material.

The Buddhist Scriptures are very extensive. In the first place, there is not one Buddhist canon, but many. If one takes only the Pali or Southern Canon, in comparison with the New Testament it is enormously greater. And if he compares it only with the Gospels—which are the chief, though not the only source of knowledge about Jesus—the disparity on a quantative basis is still greater. But in addi-

tion to the Pali, there are other canons, which, while dupli-
cating much that the former contains, add a great deal
to it.

There is no one connected story of the life of the Buddha
in the canon. There are non-canonical accounts, such as
the *Lalita-Vistara*, which may be said to be something of
a legendary life, and there are canonical accounts of some
portions of the life. But it is a very complicated task to
work through the Buddhist material and to separate out fact
from legend. Also, to determine which of the many recorded dialogues and sayings of the Buddha may really be
attributed to him presents many difficulties. The task of
the Christian scholar is simple in comparison.

Jesus' entire recorded utterances can be printed in a
comparatively small volume. Merely the longer discourses
of the Buddha run to three volumes; those of medium
length, to two volumes, while the Jataka-tales run to six
volumes.

Both figures came into the world, according to the
legendary lives, in fulfillment of a prophecy of their coming. The Christian is, of course, well aware of the Old
Testament expectation of a Messiah, which they believe
the coming of Jesus fulfills. But, equally, legend in
Buddhism foretells the Buddha's coming.

According to one account, Gautama in a previous birth
decided to become a Buddha. He was then born into one
of the heavens, where he remained until his earthly birth,
in his last human existence. The gods announce that a new
Buddha is to come. He thereupon makes five investigations
as to time, continent, country, family, and mother, and,
apparently satisfied, descends to earth and is born in Kapilavatthu to Queen Maya. Both came into the world in a
miraculous way, without benefit of human father. The

story of the annunciation to Mary is too familiar to require repeating here. That of the Buddha is less well-known. As told in the *Nidanakatha*, it runs something like this:

At the time of a certain festival, Queen Maya, having been prepared for seven days, celebrated the festival without intoxicants and with garlands and perfumes. Having ceremonially bathed, given alms, and properly adorned herself, she took the *uposatha* vows, entered her bed-chamber, lay down alone, and had a marvelous dream.

Four great kings lifted her bed and transported it to the Himalayas and placed it beneath a vast sal tree. Their queens took her to a sacred lake and bathed her to remove human stain, dressed her in heavenly raiment, anointed her with perfumes and bedecked her with flowers. In a golden mansion they prepared a divine bed with the head toward the east, and laid her on it.

Now the Boddhisatta, or Buddha-to-be, took the form of a white elephant and approached the mansion where she lay, from the north. In his trunk he held a white lotus flower. Trumpeting, he entered, circled three times around his mother's bed, struck her right side, and appeared to enter her womb.

The next day the queen awoke and told her husband the dream. He at once called sixty-four brahmins and asked them the meaning of the dream. To which they replied: "Do not be afraid, O king, the queen has conceived a male, and thou shalt have a son. If he dwells in a house, he will become a king, a universal monarch; if he leaves this house and goes forth into the world, he will become a Buddha, a remover in the world of the veil of ignorance."

Then a great earthquake followed, and thirty-two other signs appeared heralding the occurrence of something very unusual. The blind had their sight restored, the deaf heard, the lame walked, and all the fires of all the hells were extinguished.

Ten months the queen carried her precious burden. According to some legends, the Buddha could be seen within his mother's womb, and he even preached from thence, very effectively. When the time of her delivery approached, she asked the king that she be allowed to go to the home of her family. He made ready the road, adorned it with trees and flowers, flags and banners, and she set out, borne by a thousand courtiers in a golden palanquin with a huge retinue following her.

At the Lumbini gardens, which were on the road, she asked to stop. The company entered the grove, and she paused at the foot of a great sal tree. A branch reached down, and she took it in her hand. As she did so, the birth throes began. As told by Sir Edwin Arnold in the *Light of Asia*, which follows one of the legendary accounts:

> The conscious tree bent down its boughs to make
> A bower about Queen Maya's majesty,
> And earth put forth a thousand sudden flowers
> To spread a couch, while, ready for the bath,
> The rock, hard by, gave out a limpid stream
> Of crystal flow. So brought she forth her child,
> Pangless—he having on his perfect form
> The marks, thirty and two, of blessed birth.[1]

Another account has it that she was delivered standing, holding onto the branch of the sal tree. Four Mahabrahmas receive him in a golden net and set him before his mother crying, "Rejoice, O Queen, a mighty son has been born

---

[1] Book I. This poem has appeared in numerous editions, both in England and in America.

to thee." Then, though specifically declaring that he was born without any stain of impure matter, as he stepped down from his mother like a preacher of the Doctrine descending from the seat of Doctrine, he stretched out his two hands and feet quite unstained and unsoiled by any impurity, like a jewel laid on Benares cloth, and two streams of water fell from the sky and performed the regular ablutions on the bodies of son and mother. Robed in rich and soft antelope skin, he stood and looked at the world. Gods and men then worshipped him, crying, "Great being there is none like thee, much less superior anywhere." He, having examined all the quarters of the world and seeing no one superior to himself, took seven steps and cried in a lordly voice, "I am the chief in the world."

Queen Maya, the mother of the newborn babe, lived only seven days after his birth, and he was reared by his mother's sister, Mahaprajapati. Was his birth thus a virgin birth as related of Jesus? E. J. Thomas says of it, "This is not properly a virgin birth, but it may be called parthenogenetic, that is, Suddhodana was not his progenitor."[2] That sounds like, "Well, yes and no," or, rather, "No and yes." Thomas goes on to say that the oldest accounts of his birth seem to presuppose nothing unusual about it. He was, to be sure, well-born, reference being made to the ancestors on both his father's and his mother's side for seven generations back, but only in the way that kings are supposed to be born. Certainly the legendary lives leave one with the impression that it was a very unusual birth. But beyond the effect of enhancing, possibly, the importance of the

---

[2] E. J. Thomas, *The Life of Buddha as Legend and History* (New York: Alfred A. Knopf, Inc., 1927).

Buddha thus, there are no doctrines of a theological nature, of which I am aware, that grow out of it.

Both Jesus and Buddha are recognized soon after birth by elder religious figures as of unusual significance and destined to have a great influence upon humanity. In the case of Jesus, on the occasion of the presentation in the temple, the child was seen by Simeon, to whom, Luke relates, it had been revealed by the Holy Spirit that he should not die until he had seen the coming of the Christ. The ancient, lifting up his voice, prayed, "Now let thy servant depart in peace, for mine eyes have seen thy salvation . . . a light for revelation to the Gentiles and for glory to thy people Israel."

At the birth of Buddha, the great sage Asita, meditating in the Himalayas, beheld many wonders. According to legend, he rose up like a royal swan and flew to Kapilavatthu and came to the house of the king. Invited to enter, he asked to see the child, and observing that he bore the thirty-two marks of a great man and the eighty minor marks, and with a glory surpassing by a thousandfold that of the world-protectors, he cried: "Marvelous verily is this person that has appeared in the world!" Then, circling about the child and contemplating his person, he exclaimed: "If he dwells in a house, he will become a king, a universal monarch . . . but if he goes forth from a house to a houseless life, he will become a Tathagatha, loudly proclaimed, a fully enlightened Buddha," and, looking upon the child, he wept.

"Why do you weep?" asked Suddhodana, "Is there misfortune for the boy?"

To which Asita replied: "I weep not for the lad, for him there will be no misfortune, but I weep for myself. . . .

This boy will without doubt attain complete enlightenment, and, having done so, will take countless beings across the ocean of transmigration to the other side and establish them in the immortal state. But we shall not see that Buddha-jewel. Hence, O king, I weep . . . for I shall not be able to reverence him."[3]

This story, that of the unusual birth, and others have impressed some scholars so that they have come to believe that Buddhism influenced Christianity, and that some of the Gospel stories go back in their origins to Buddhism. They trace out the line of influence as coming through the Essenes, an ascetic group in Palestine who they think were strongly under Buddhist influence, this having come to the Near East through the missionaries whom Asoka sent out to the west during his reign. While this must always be regarded as a possibility, I have personally never been convinced by the so-called evidence that there was any substantial support for the view.

As in the case of Jesus, there is little in the canonical literature of Buddhism concerning the life of Buddha between the time of his birth and the great renunciation. Concerning Jesus there is the story of the boy Jesus in the temple talking with the elders. The literature of Buddhism does give, purportedly in Buddha's own words, something concerning the life of luxury which he led as a young prince. "Night and day a white parasol was held over me so that I should not be touched by cold or heat, by dust or weeds or dew. I had three palaces," etc.[4] But in the non-canonical literature, there is a vast wealth of story concern-

---

[3] *Ibid.*, pp. 40–41. Paraphrased from the prose version in the *Lalita-vistara*.

[4] *Anguttara*, 1:145.

ing him. When he was taken to be taught writing, he asks
the master which of sixty-four scripts he is going to teach
him, some of them quite unknown to the master himself.
When the time comes for him to marry, according to a
late source, the father of Gopa, who was most beautiful
and good of all those who presented themselves for his
choice, demanded that he prove himself worthy in a con-
test with other aspirants for her hand. Gautama won easily
in writing and in mathematics, but he must also prove his
physical prowess. This he did at running, at jumping, at
wrestling, and, finally, in archery, using a famous bow
which none but he was able to string. When the elephant
on which he was to ride in triumph through the city was
struck dead by one of his opponents, Gautama touched it
with his foot, and it stood up and paid him homage.[5] Somewhat similar wonder stories are told of Jesus in the New
Testament Apocrypha; for example, the boy Jesus restores
a broken water pot on one occasion, and makes clay birds,
which He has playfully formed, come to life and fly away.

The wealth and pleasures Gautama enjoyed are detailed
at great length in various of the non-canonical sources—all
doubtless in order to enhance the importance of his act
of renunciation. His marriage was most happy. He lacked
nothing in the way of pleasure and companionship and
beauty and devotion, all of which should have kept him
contented. But he was not content. Even when a son was
born to him, he felt there was something lacking. He grew
restive at his virtual confinement in the palace grounds. He
wanted to see the world outside.

Reluctantly his father consented, but care was taken to

---

[5] A. F. Herold, *Life of Buddha*, translated by Paul C. Blum (New York:
Albert & Charles Boni, Inc., 1927), pp. 44–47.

decorate the city, through which he would ride, with garlands, and to see to it that nothing that was ugly or old or
evil was visible. So the Prince rode forth in a golden
chariot, and saw everywhere only youth and beauty and
wealth. He rejoiced in it and in the warmth of the welcome
the people gave him. But the gods, as one of the sources
had it, set an old man, worn out and decrepit, leaning
heavily on his staff, in one of the streets, and the Prince
saw him. He had never before seen old age. He did not
understand.

"What is this I see?" he asked his charioteer.

"That is an old man, sire," the charioteer replied.

"Do all men grow old? And shall I too?" he asked.

"Ay, sire, you too, for all men grow old."

"Back to the palace," ordered the Prince. Over his life
a shadow had fallen.

Again he drove forth, and yet again, once seeing sickness, then death. The shadow deepened. He pondered
much on old age, sickness, and death. Nothing his father
could do by way of increasing the sources of pleasure and
joy could move him. A dream of Gopa which terrorized
her seemed to him an omen of good. He wandered forth
in the fields. There he met a monk, sent by the gods, and
in conversation with him suddenly knew what he must do.
He sought out the king, and told him that he must leave
the palace and seek deliverance. The king was shocked
and sought by every means to dissuade him, but in vain.
"Promise me, father," he cried, "that my life will not end
in death, that sickness shall not come, nor old age, and that
misfortune shall not take away my possessions, and I will
stay." The king could give him no such assurance. Gautama's mind was therefore made up. He would leave his

home, his family, everything, and go out into the world
in search of a way to triumph over these evils. That night
he did so, riding away on his faithful charger, Kanthaka,
after a last look at his sleeping wife and son, in quest of
the way of release from what had come to seem to him the
universal suffering to which mankind was subject. "To
this city I shall not return," he said as he rode away, "until
I have seen the end of life and death."

But how should he find the sought-for release? He did
not know, but he first became an ascetic, of which there
were many in India in his time.

Most of this story is legend rather than sober fact, but
that there was a renunciation of some kind, around which
these legends are built, is undoubtedly true. As a matter
of fact, most Buddhist scholars are agreed that, while the
wealth and the magnificence of his father are certainly
legendary, there does underlie the myths the fact that
Buddha was the son of a ruler of a small north central
province of India, and that he did abandon his home and
the succession to his father's rule and seek release from the
universal suffering of man, or, to put it in Christian theological language, salvation.

His leaving home behind to undertake this quest was not
at all unusual. This was quite a common practice. First one
went through the student stage. Then householder, during
which period marriage and rearing a family were the accepted practice. Generally it was not until one had reached
middle age or later and had provided for his family that the
Hindu left home, first to become a forest-dweller or hermit;
then finally a Holy Man or Mendicant, who cut himself
loose from all family ties and became a begger, intent upon
only one thing, release or *moksha*. Gautama had already

attained the householder stage. It was his so early abandonment of this stage that was unusual. He is said to have been
only twenty-nine years of age when this occurred.

Like Jesus, he was tempted. Mara, the Buddhist tempter,
appears more than once, in the various sources. At the very
opening of the gate of the city that he might depart, Mara
appeared, promising that on the seventh day he would become ruler over four great islands and two hundred small
ones if he would not leave. But Buddha refused to listen.
Accounts differ as to how he spent the years before attaining enlightenment. However, they agree fairly well that
he became an ascetic and with great rigor practiced asceticism, hoping, perhaps as did the Jains, that through such
self-mortification he might win release. He certainly
omitted no form of austerity commonly practiced in India,
but to no avail. He finally swooned away of weakness,
and his disciples—for he had a following of other ascetics
—thought that he was dead. But, returning to consciousness, he took food and abandoned completely his ascetic
practices, convinced that salvation did not lie in that direction. At last he resolved that he would sit in meditation
beneath the famous Bo tree, not rising until he had reached
enlightenment. "Even if my skin should parch, even if my
hand should wither, even if my bones should crumble into
dust, until I have attained supreme knowledge I shall not
move from this seat," he said in a solemn voice, and crossed
his legs.[6]

Then Mara, sensing that here lay a great threat to himself, gathered his armies and advanced to destroy him. On
another occasion, Mara had appealed to his desire for pleasure or power. A favorite device was to send a most beauti-

---

[6] *Ibid.*, p. 96.

ful and attractive young woman to seduce one who had
become a monk or a hermit—and sometimes the device
worked. Later Buddha's enemies sought to do just that. But
here, as told in the *Lalita-vistara*, the attempt was more
dramatic. First Mara sought to frighten Gautama. He un-
leashed the fury of the winds against him, devastating
homes and villages, but not even his robe was disarranged.
Then came the rains, flooding cities, but not a drop affected
him. Blazing rocks hurled at him could not touch him.
They fell at his feet and became flowers. Mara's army
hurled javelins and shot clouds of arrows at him, but all
weapons, swords, battle-axes, all, fell at his feet and changed
to flowers. Mara's soldiers, affrighted at such proof of their
impotence, fled, and Mara was totally defeated. He wept,
bitterly.

It may be noted that the attack of Mara here precedes
enlightenment. That of Jesus at the hand of Satan came
after His baptism. Both very evidently went through deep
struggles of soul before finally accepting the role each was
destined to play.

The enlightenment experience, which was the turning
point in Buddha's career, left Gautama—now the Buddha
—with the sure conviction that he had found the way of
deliverance. His quest, for which he had sacrificed everything, was ended. Henceforth he was to go up and down
north central India teaching the way to others. However
it may be explained, psychologically or otherwise, it was
one of those great moments in history pregnant with meaning for the world of humanity. All the Orient has been
different because of what happened under that sacred tree.
Perhaps half the total population of the world has been
affected in some measure by it, and the end is not yet.

In the forty years of his subsequent ministry of teaching, Buddha expressed in various ways what happened there. Best-known and simplest, perhaps, was his account in what is called the First Sermon at Benares. Here he sets forth the content of his insight gained in the enlightenment experience in systematic fashion, generally known as the Four Noble Truths and the Eightfold Path. Told very simply, it runs thus. Suffering is universal. This is the first of the Four Truths. "Decay is suffering, sickness is suffering, death is suffering; likewise Sorrow, Grief, Woe, Lamentation, Despair." But suffering has its origin in *Craving*. The Sanskrit or Pali word is variously translated as grasping, craving, thirst, desire. It is difficult to express it in a word. There is in it an element of insistence; not just desire, but passionate desire. It is, he says, "that craving which leads downwards to birth—the craving for sensation, the craving to be born again, the craving to have done with rebirth." It is clear here that Buddha takes his start within the framework of Hinduism, where the belief in the cycle of rebirth was a constant factor. To many, the desire to escape the wheel of existence had become the very quest of religion itself. It is interesting to discover many modern Mahayana Buddhists insisting that Buddha didn't really believe in rebirth or transmigration at all. But here it is unmistakably set forth in the most basic statement of the way to enlightenment.

Thus far there was nothing essentially new in his analysis, nor was his Third Truth, which is the gospel of Buddhism, wholly new. There is a way out of suffering. It lies in the "utter passionless cessation of, the giving up, the forsaking, the release from, the absence of longing for, this craving." But how is this practically possible? It is the

Fourth Truth that is Buddha's real contribution. It is the way leading to the cessation of suffering, the Eightfold Path —often called the Middle Path. As one reads it, particularly the first five of the eight steps, he is struck with its plain common sense and practical character. It consists of right views, right aims, right speech, right action, right living. So far, it is eminently down-to-earth. The final three steps look in the direction of the more intellectual and mystical techniques of the Hindu yogins. These are right effort, right mindfulness, right contemplation.

Here is the heart of Buddhism—at least, early Buddhism, and the Buddhism of the Southern or Hinayana school.

Obviously, when one speaks of *right* views, *right* aims, and so forth, it becomes necessary to inquire what is meant by *right*. What are the right views? Fortunately, the Buddha answers this in one of the longer discourses.[7]

Right views are the knowledge about ill or suffering, its cause, and the manner of its cessation, that is, the Four Noble Truths view. And so on he goes, defining in specific terms what is meant. The next four are eminently moral in character—fairly well summed up in the Five Commandments of Buddhism against lying, stealing, drinking, sexual irregularities, and killing. By "killing" he means taking life, period, whether human or subhuman.

Thus far, the path is open to all men of whatever age or class, the layman as well as the monk. The sixth might still apply to such: right effort, which he defines as "generating the will to inhibit the arising of evil, immoral conditions, and to cause the arising of good conditions that have not yet arisen." But when he goes on to right mindfulness and right contemplation, which latter he describes as abiding

---

[7] *Digha Nikaya*, ii, 312.

successive "trances," reaching finally the fourth, which is a state of "perfect purity of balance and equanimity," he has clearly gone beyond what is possible for the layman. Indeed, it is not without significance to note, as Woodward does,[8] that Buddha calls those on the first five steps of the path *disciples*; those on the last three, *brothers*. That is, it becomes an ideal for one who forsakes the common life to give himself up wholly to the pursuit of the goal of liberation.

Now, since this is a comparative study, note, first, that in all this there is not one single reference of any kind to anything outside one's self to which one may appeal or upon which one may in any way depend for the attainment of the goal he seeks. This way of salvation is an out-and-out self-operating system. Man apparently can and, indeed, must depend upon himself in his effort to attain birthlessness, which elsewhere appears to be the definition of salvation. Nirvana, about which it is difficult to say anything very definite, though many different similes are used to describe it, seems always to mean that state from which there is no return to birth.

That is to say, Buddhism, as here set forth, makes no place whatever for God. I do not mean to say that Buddha did not believe in God. Certainly in the Buddhist literature, even the canonical books, Buddha refers to the gods as though they exist; but at the deepest level of man's need, in the most important quest he undertakes, for Buddha God has no part to play at all. This is a point of profound difference of outlook between the two great figures.

The seeking and the finding are the important things in

---

[8] F. L. Woodward, translator, *Some Sayings of the Buddha* (London: Humphrey Milford, Oxford University Press, 1925), p. 13.

Buddha's teaching. When questioners seek to draw him out on questions of a theoretical nature, he refuses to enter into discussion with them. He will not be deflected from the main concern, which is how to reach Arhantship or Nirvana. Whatever does not conduce to this end does not interest him.

Does Buddha have no conception of an underlying reality back of all phenomena? If he does, he does not state it clearly or unambiguously, for highly divergent philosophies have grown out of his reputed utterances. In contrast to this, consider the simple, naive faith of Jesus, taken, of course, from a non-speculative Jewish background. Here we find the belief, of course, in God, the creator and orderer of the world. He is personal. He enters into relationship with man. He hears and answers prayers. He loves mankind, he is compassionate and forgiving—although also a God of judgment. He is concerned with man's salvation. Jesus thinks of himself as sent of God to call man to repentance and to a right relationship with God.

It is with the Kingdom of God that He is chiefly concerned, and while He nowhere defines it in unequivocal terms, He is all the time seeking to tell men what it is like, and to induce them to meet the requirements of membership in that Kingdom. It is the most important thing in life. "Seek ye first the Kingdom of God . . . and all these things shall be added unto you."

Both men had a profound sense of mission which drove them. In the case of Jesus, it took Him to the cross in an incredibly short time and He yielded His life in what must have appeared to many of his contemporaries as a manifest failure. "I must work the works of him that sent me while it is yet day." "The son of man came to seek and to save that which was lost." "The son of Man came not to be ministered unto, but to minister and to give his life as ransom for many," may reflect a theological explanation of the effect of His death which Jesus Himself did not share; but that He felt driven to give His life that man might be saved seems clearly indicated, not only by these words, but others, and, more than by words, by what He did. Surely He did not seek death as an escape: "If possible let this cup pass from me" seems a perfectly natural prayer on his lips —"Nevertheless, not my will but thine be done" seems just as certainly and naturally to describe what He did and the mood in which He did it.

In Buddha's case, his sense of a mission kept him preaching up and down north central India for a period of some forty years after he had himself attained release, as he believed. Why? If birth is evil, if escape from rebirth is the ultimate good after which men seek, why, when it was within his grasp, did he not claim it? Or if, as would have been the case in his thought, any act to hasten the dissolution of the body would have been considered evil, why not give himself, as had been the usual custom of those solitary seekers, to the enjoyment of solitude and meditation, reaching the state of *samadhi*, which is an early foretaste of what Nirvana really is? But he did not. Instead, he walked India's dusty roads during the dry seasons and put up in some sacred grove during the period of the rains, tirelessly teaching and preaching release to India's people.

It is said of Jesus that He had compassion upon the multitudes. A recent writer on Buddhism entitled his book, *Buddhism, a Religion of Infinite Compassion*.[9] He was writing, not simply of Buddha, but of the fully developed

---

[9] Edited by Clarence H. Hamilton (New York: Liberal Arts Press, 1952).

Mahayana. Yet, how account for Buddha's ministry on any other basis than that he, too, felt compassion? He is described as one "born into the world for the good of the many, for the happiness of the many, for the advantage, the good, the happiness of gods and men, out of compassion for the world."[10] Hamilton describes Buddha as "an example of profound compassion, of limitless unselfish devotion to the highest welfare of others." He further points out that, in the Jatakas or Birth Stories, his final birth and his enlightenment were due to the accumulated merit resulting from his "marvelous heroic deeds of self-renouncing service."[11]

Both Jesus and Buddha sent out their disciples to preach their gospel to others. The Great Commission of Jesus is too well-known to need repeating here. That of Buddha is less familiar. At a time when it was said there were but sixty-four Arhats in the world; that is, at a comparatively early period in his ministry, Buddha sent his disciples out, saying to them: "Go ye forth, brethern, on your journey, for the profit of the many, for the bliss of the many, out of compassion for the world, for the welfare, the profit of *devas* and mankind. Go not any two together, proclaim the Norm, goodly in the beginning, in the middle—in the end. Both in the spirit and in the letter, do ye make known the all-perfected, utterly pure, righteous life. There are beings—perishing through not hearing the Norm. There will be some who will understand."[12] Observe here also the note of compassion—"out of compassion for the world."

---

[10] *Digha Nikaya*, 5. J. B. Pratt, *The Pilgrimage of Buddhism* (New York: The Macmillan Company, 1927). Used by permission of the publishers.

[11] Hamilton, *op. cit.*, p. xvii.

[12] *Vinaya*, 1.21, Woodward, *op. cit.*, p. 30.

Although it is not here specifically stated, the primary aim of the Buddha was to lead men to Arhatship, and to attain to this, it was necessary to enter the order. The attainment of Nirvana in this life through the following of the Eightfold Path requires full-time effort, and is impossible for the layman. It is to this extent world-fleeing, and stands in sharp contrast to Jesus' teaching, which finds expression in His prayer, "I pray not that **thou** shouldst take them out of the world but that thou shouldst keep them from the evil one"—presumably right in the world in which they lived and worked. To "wander alone like a rhinoceros" is pictured by the Buddha as the Buddhist ideal of monkhood. "Without covetousness, deceit, craving, having gotten rid of passion and folly, being free from desire in all the world, let one wander alone like a rhinoceros. Having left son and wife, father and mother, wealth and corn, and relatives, the different objects of desire, let me wander alone like a rhinoceros."[13]

To be sure, Jesus said, "He who loves father or mother or son or daughter more than me is not worthy of me, and he who does not take up his cross and follow me is not worthy of me." But that has not generally been interpreted as monastic in meaning. Nor did Jesus found or perpetuate any community that set itself apart from the world about it. Jesus taught of the Kingdom of God, which seemed now to be the present and again to be future, and to the early Christians generally seemed to be thought of as being fulfilled on an other-worldly plane. But it did not take them out of the common life of their times. In loyalty to their beliefs concerning Jesus and His teaching, they did

---

[13] *Sutta-Nipata*, translated by V. Fausböll, *Sacred Books of the East* (London: Oxford University Press, 1881), Vol. X, p. 9.

refuse to participate in some of the activities of society. They would not take oaths; and could therefore not serve as magistrates, and they would not engage in war. But they lived within the normal community, married, had families, and carried on the ordinary daily tasks involved in making a living. Celibacy did not become a rule for the clergy until several centuries had passed.

Yet Buddha, like Jesus, did perform a ministry to laymen as well as monks. To the laymen, he taught the ordinary virtues of honesty, purity, kindness, sobriety, non-killing, and so forth. In a memorable passage, he said: "There are three odors that travel with the wind and not against it, but there is only one sweet odor that travels both against the wind and with it, the sweet odor of a man or woman living in a village or a town who has taken the Buddha, the Dhamma and the Sangha as his guides, who refrains from killing, stealing, adultery, lying, and strong drink, who is religious and virtuous, who lives the life of the householder with thoughts devoid of avarice and is liberal in giving."[14] The five precepts, which are not to lie, steal, be unchaste, take life, or drink intoxicants, are incumbent upon the layman as well as the monk; but, unless he forsakes the common life and becomes a monk, he cannot hope to attain enlightenment in his present life span. However, since life does not end with death, but returns to birth again and again and again, he is not therefore lost to Nirvana if he does not at once attain it. Buddha also speaks of the layman as attaining the state of a "never returner," who may be born into a higher heaven and there eventually achieve enlightenment.[15]

---

14 Pratt, *op. cit.*, *Anguttara* III, 79, p. 47.
15 *Ibid.*, p. 47. See further in Neumann's *Majjhima* II, p. 320.

If at these points Buddha and Jesus differ markedly, there are other points at which they seem to be in substantial agreement.

"Hatred does not cease by hatred at any time; hatred ceases by love. This is an old rule,"[16] said Buddha.

"I say unto you: Love your enemies, pray for those who persecute you," said Jesus. (Matt. 5:44.)

"Let a man overcome anger by love; let him overcome evil by good; let him overcome the greedy by liberality, the liar by truth," said the Buddha.[17]

Jesus said: "Ye have heard it said of old times, 'An eye for an eye and a tooth for a tooth,' but I say unto you: Do not resist one who is evil. But if anyone strikes you on the right cheek, turn to him the other also, if he . . . take away your coat, let him have your cloak as well; and if anyone forces you to go one mile, go with him two miles." (Matt. 5:38-41.)

Purna, one of his disciples, once sought permission of the Buddha to go on a mission to a distant and dangerous people. But, said the Buddha, "these are violent, cruel, and furious men. When they get angry and curse you, what will you think?"

"I will think," he answered, "that they are kind and good men, . . . they who are angry and curse me but do not beat me with their hands or stones."

"But if they do beat you?" Then he would think them good that they did not use clubs and swords. If they did this, he would think them good and kind that they did not kill him. But, said the Buddha, "What if they do kill you?" Then replied Purna, "I will certainly think that

---

[16] *Dhammapada* I, 5, translated by Max Müller, *Sacred Books of the East* (London: Oxford University Press, 1881), Vol. X.

[17] *Ibid., Dhammapada* XVII, 3.

they are kind and good since they deliver me with so little pain from this vile body."

"Go," said the Buddha, "yourself delivered, deliver others: yourself arrived at the other shore, bring others there; yourself having attained Nirvana, conduct others to it." [18]

Jesus, of course, taught, "Thou shalt not kill," but not only this—which of old had been taught them. "Everyone who is angry with his brother shall be liable to judgment," said He.

Buddha went farther at this point than Jesus and extended his prohibition of killing to the sub-human world as well. In his doctrine of *ahimsa* or non-killing, he went far beyond the Hinduism of his day. In so doing, he gave a direction of Buddhism which has made it forever shun force and violence as a method of its spread, a claim that can be made neither by Christianity nor by Islam. Although unfortunately Buddhists, like Christians, have allowed the state to use them in the mutual slaughter of war, often enough without any sense of moral strain, and only infrequently over their expressed protest against it. Buddhism has an even firmer pacifist basis than has Christianity. One cannot help wondering what would have happened if both Buddhism and Christianity had kept faith with their founders in the matter of non-violence. Both founders were deeply convinced that the victories of the world were to be won by spiritual rather than material means. Were they right? Maybe they were, and we stand on the brink of a world war too frightful to contemplate, with the power literally to destroy our world, only because we would not listen to their counsel.

---

[18] Pratt, *op. cit., Majjhima* 145, p. 54.

Indeed, in their whole practical ethical teaching, it is clear that these two amazing figures are in essential agreement. If there is any conspicuous virtue taught by Jesus which the Buddha omitted, I am not aware of it. It is true that their theoretical ethical bases differ. That of the Buddha was completely non-theistic. That of Christianity has a firm theistic base. But both agreed that there is a moral order in the universe, something which supports the good and exacts penalty for the doing of evil.

In the case of the Buddha, it is an inexorable impersonal but cosmic law, Karma, the law of the deed, the law of retribution, which operates. In the case of Jesus, it is the law of an infinitely good, but just, personal God, the Father, just but forgiving and loving, who seeks man's good. And in the case of the Buddha, there is no one to help. Man must work out his salvation alone, relying solely upon his own effort. In Christianity, as based upon Jesus and His teaching, God takes the initiative in seeking man's redemption, and sends His Son as mediator to effect it. More may have been read into Jesus' part in the process than He Himself would have asserted, or even allowed. Yet there are numerous sayings in the Gospels to the effect that it is His mission to call men to repentance and entrance into the Kingdom of God. "The Son of a Man came to seek and to save the lost." (Luke 19:10) "I am come that they may have life and have it abundantly." (John 10:10)

For the one who sought immediate release from the whole of existence, a rigorousness of discipline was required in Buddhism that went far beyond anything contemplated in Jesus' teaching, certainly as I read it. There was, even in the Middle Path of the Buddha, an ascetic quality of life which is foreign to the New Testament, although a monasticism has developed within Christianity which approaches the Buddhist practice.

The Buddha's general attitude toward the body, its appetites, and its desires is far more rigorous than that of Jesus. To be sure, the latter spoke of the "lust of the flesh," and asserted, "If thine eye offend thee, pluck it out." But there is nothing in Jesus' utterances to equal, for example, Buddha's "graveyard meditation." The attitude of the Buddha toward women stands in sharpest contrast to that of Jesus. To the Buddha, they are always inferior to men —a snare and a threat to men. Reluctantly he permitted them to found an order, but declared pessimistically that they would bring about the eventual disruption of the Sangha five hundred years earlier than it would otherwise occur.[19]

Love has been singled out as the primary element in Jesus' teaching. The Gospel of John and the Epistles of John are full of emphasis upon this quality. But Buddha likewise stresses love. J. B. Pratt, who has given what seems to me to be the best analysis of the ethical teachings of the Buddha, finds him distinguishing three attitudes which are all expressed by the English word *love*: sexual lust; tender personal affection, which tends to make one's peace dependent on the presence or at least the welfare of the beloved; and earnest, even tender, goodwill of an impersonal sort for all. Buddha condemns the first, regards the second as leading to a sense of sorrow or loss, but thoroughly approves only the third. Pratt's discussion, written before the current custom of distinguishing between "eros" and "agape," is really doing just that. The Christian "agape," as it is used in the famous passage in 1 Corinthians, 13, he

---

[19] Herold, *op. cit.*, p. 228.

says, is akin to the Buddhist-approved sense of love. Now abideth faith, hope, love—*agape*— a "universal and impersonal, yet tender good will." [20]

We must conclude this chapter with a brief look at the way in which Buddhists came to think of Buddha. In Buddhism, as in Christianity, what people did actually come to think of their founder has probably had a greater influence upon their formal thought structure or theology than did his teachings.

Now, the Buddha lived a long time. He grew old, outlived many of his followers, and long before his death had come to be looked upon with veneration by them. After his death, it was only a little while before they were venerating his relics and building *stupas, dagobas, pagodas* to house them. Today in Kandy, Ceylon, is to be found the famous *tooth* temple, where a tooth of the venerable one is treasured. Another temple is built about a hair from his head. Statues of Buddha began to be made, usually in the meditative posture, seated upon a lotus pedestal.

Nevertheless, so consistently had the Buddha inculcated in his followers the idea of the utter necessity of depending upon their own efforts that Southern or Hinayana Buddhism, at the higher intellectual level at least, has insisted until now that no one can help one—that he must work out his own salvation. To be sure, there are Buddha statues in the temples, and people are to be seen in large numbers before these figures. Why do they do this? Solely, they claim, for the subjective benefits that accrue to them in the practice. It is undoubtedly a help to concentration. Pratt calls this subjective worship at its purest. I strongly suspect that the simple layman here prays to the Buddha very much as simple folk the world over do to

[20] *Ibid.*, p. 52.

the gods, great or small, knowing nothing of the fine distinctions drawn by psychologists and theologians. This form of Buddhism is found chiefly in Ceylon, Burma, Thailand, and some other sections of southeastern Asia. Gautama, the Buddha, is central to Hinayana Buddhism, although even there, there exists a belief in other Buddhas.

But Buddhism as it took form in northern India and spread through Tibet, China, Korea, and Japan, developed in a quite different fashion. Owing almost certainly in part to the highly polytheistic environment in which it developed there, and owing to the fact that many of those who came into Buddhism were accustomed to a plurality of divinities, the development of the idea of many Buddhas seems quite natural. And in this process *the* Buddha tends to drop out of the center and to become but one of a vast number of Buddhas. The Buddha had gone through many births before he arrived finally at Enlightenment and entered Nirvana at the close of his life span. It eventually came to be believed that everyone was a potential Buddha, and the ultimate goal of Buddhism came to be just the attaining of Buddhahood. This was the "great career"— one translation of the name given to the Northern Buddhists, *Mahayana*—though more frequently it is translated as the "great vehicle" as opposed to *Hinayana*, the "little vehicle." It was great in that it opened the way more widely to the achievement of its goal than the narrow way of the monk, who must, in the nature of things, always be one of a small minority group.

The career leading to full Buddhahood consisted eventually of ten separate stages. One who was on the way to Buddhahood, that is, who had taken the vow to become one, was known as a *Bodhisattva* or *Bodhisatta*. And probably owing to the influence of Hindu *bhakti* or devotional

Hinduism, these Bodhisattvas were eventually conceived of as a kind of cosmic helpers who could be called upon by others farther back on the way to aid them in their progress toward the goal. This was, of course, a fundamental change from the stern self-salvation system of Hinayana or Southern Buddhism.

In the popular Mahayana sects, known as the Pure Land sects, even the ultimate ideal for Buddhahood is pretty well lost sight of and the aspiration of the devotee is to reach the Pure Land or Western Paradise, which is in many respects not unlike the Christian heaven. Buddhism had, of course, fallen heir to the multitudinous heavens and hells of Hinduism, and the one on the way to Nirvana might, for his sins or his good deeds, be born into one of the many hells or heavens. But here in the Western Paradise is an ideal which leaves little to be desired to the common man, who may never aspire to anything beyond it, although the instructed might look upon it as only one stage on the way to salvation or Buddhahood. For those aspiring to the Western Paradise, it is Amida, or Amitabha, who becomes effectively the savior divinity through whose grace and merit, if properly called upon, the soul may hope to gain it. Here the likeness to the development in Christianity is very close. But this is not *the* Buddha, Sakyamuni. He is of little or no importance to such sectarians. I suppose that this is somewhat akin to a substantial segment of the Christian world whose preoccupation with the original historic Jesus is very slight, but who speak of *the Christ* as one quite different, who may have appeared in the historic person of Jesus but is not limited to that appearance.

In these Northern popular sects, the Buddha—or rather, the Buddhas—are frankly worshipped, not merely subjectively, but as gods everywhere are. The prayers to those figures are as warmly intimate sometimes as are those of the orthodox Christian to Christ, whom he thinks of as God. Although Sakyamuni or Gautama Buddha is one of the five great Buddhas, in the popular sects it is Amitabha-Omito-fu, Amida, who is the Savior. He began, as a monk, the career of Bodhisattva, took forty-two vows, and at last became a Buddha after attaining assurance that all who call upon his name would be saved. It is through his vicarious suffering and goodness that salvation is possible. Merit is transferred, as in Christianity, through faith to the believer who calls upon him.

While this seems undoubtedly to be far away from the original teaching of Buddhism, with its stern emphasis upon self-effort, it is interpreted by so great a Mahayana scholar as Suzuki as "the logical outcome of enlightenment consciousness." Certainly this spirit is found in the Bod-hisattva ideal in Mahayana. And it is these who are wor-shipped more than the Buddhas. The spirit of yearning to help others is nowhere more beautifully expressed than by Santi-deva in *The Path of Light.*

"I would fain become a soother of all sorrows of all creatures. May I be a balm to the sick, a healer and servitor, until sickness come never again; may I be an unfailing store for the poor, and serve them with manifold things for their need. My own being and my pleasures, all my righteous-ness in the past, present, and future, I surrender indiffer-ently that all creatures may win to their end. . . . I would be a protector of the unprotected, a guide for wayfarers, a ship, a dyke, and a bridge for them who seek the further shore; a lamp for them who need a lamp, a bed for them who need a bed; a slave for them who need a slave." [21]

If points of difference between Buddha and Jesus be-

---

[21] Quoted in Pratt, *op. cit.*, p. 219.

yond those already mentioned are sought, at least two are noteworthy: (1) the clear teaching by Jesus of personal immortality. While no blueprint for the hereafter is given, He taught definitely the existence of a soul which would survive the crisis of death. In John He said, "I go to prepare a place for you, that where I am there ye may be also." Buddha taught, according to some, a no-soul doctrine, yet that something, a man's *karma*, goes on bringing to successive births, in some new arrangement, the basic *skandas* into which he analyzed the self, until finally release is attained from the wheel into Nirvana—a state of passionless peace. Popular thought embraced heavens and hells not unlike some Christian ideas as at least temporary rewards for one's deeds. Always both held to a moral continuity between this and whatever future form life might take.

A second radical difference between the figures was in the manner of their death. Buddha lived out a long life of ministry of some 45 years and died a natural death, probably from ptomaine poisoning. Jesus' death was upon the cross, a tragic ostensibly premature end to His earthly ministry. He died as a logical consequence of His teaching, with a prayer for forgiveness of those who had crucified Him on His lips. This act has in subsequent development of His faith almost overshadowed His life. Interpreted in terms of the ancient sacrificial system of the Hebrews, it came to be thought of as the price of man's redemption. It has become central in Christian theology, the difference between various Christian sects sometimes lying in the way in which they have rationalized the atonement.

It need hardly be said that in Buddhism nothing comparable has appeared. To be sure, the note of unselfish renunciation has played an important role in Buddhism, and in the Mahayana concept of the Bodhisattva who refuses to enter into Buddhahood unless assured that all who call upon him will be saved has some elements of the *kenosis* idea in Christian theology. But it is at best only a weak approximation to the Christian idea. A third additional point of difference lies in the emphasis in Christianity upon the element of sin and judgment. It is said that in Buddhism there is no sense of sin and guilt, and therefore no sense of forgiveness. There is a real question in my own mind as to the degree to which Jesus Himself taught this. He came preaching, to be sure, repentance, for the Kingdom of God was at hand. He came to call sinners to repentance. In the institution of the Holy Sacrament he spoke of the cup as the blood of the covenant which was poured out for many for the remission of sins. Undoubtedly he was concerned about man's sin and forgiveness, but it is in Paul that the Christian doctrine of sin is wrought out, which has been so central in Christian belief. It is not without significance that in a number of books on Buddha and Buddhism, which I picked up at random, there is no entry in the index of sin or repentance or forgiveness.

Thus we have compared two men whose lives and teachings have been of enormous influence in the life of the world. Different in many respects they undoubtedly are, and their movements have developed in very different fashion. But on some of the major questions of life, they speak with a united voice, particularly on moral questions. On the crucial question for our time—that of war and peace, they would be at one. If their followers were united on this question, and would take seriously their teachings, our world might yet be saved from the horror and destructiveness of an atomic war.

3

Jesus and Krishna

———————◻———————

MORE ALLITERATIVELY, THE TITLE OF THIS CHAPTER SHOULD be "Christ and Krishna," for it has been quite customary to put these two figures in contrast. Often Krishna has been called the Indian Christ—with what justification, our discussion may reveal. There is no founder of Hinduism. Like Topsy, it "just growed." But Krishna may well stand for at least one of the major aspects of Hinduism, and as such quite deserves a place in this series.

Krishna, then, can hardly be called a founder of religion at all. Indeed, many doubt that there ever was an historical Krishna. But others, particularly Hindus themselves, quite eminent scholars, do not hesitate to speak of him in historical terms. The outstanding philosopher of contemporary India, for example, S. Radhakrishnan, who recently translated the *Bhagavad Gita*, does not question that he actually lived. He writes of him thus: "So far as the teaching of the *Bhagavad Gita* is concerned, it is immaterial whether Krishna the teacher is an historical figure or not. The material point is the eternal incarnation of the Divine, the everlasting bringing forth of the perfect and divine life in the universe and the soul of man. There is,

– 46 –

however, ample evidence in favor of the historicity of Krishna." [1]

But there is nothing in Hinduism which presents a concise source for Krishna, such as the Gospels do for Jesus. One gathers bits of information concerning a Krishna here and there within the vast literature of ancient India, but it is not always clear that these are references to *the* Krishna. There is a Krishna in the narrative portion of the great epic, the *Mahabharata;* there is a Krishna in the *Vishnu Purana;* there is, of course, the Krishna of the much-loved *Bhagavad Gita*—the favorite Vishnuite scripture; an episode also in the *Mahabharata,* but one which is obviously not meant to be historical. Most of the time one moves in an area of legend as he seeks factual information about Krishna. About the most that can be said is that, back of and underneath the legendary Krishna, there is an individual, or possibly several individuals, who have over a long period of time been woven finally into a composite Krishna who appears as an incarnation of the great personal God, Vishnu, and speaks in the *Bhagavad Gita.*

In the *Vishnu Purana,* which is of comparatively late origin, Krishna is represented as having been brought up in a cowherd family, although he was in reality of noble birth, the son of Vasudeva and Devaki. The latter was a brother of King Kamsa. Just after the marriage of Vasudeva and Devaki, it had been prophesied that the king's death would be at the hands of his sister's eighth son. Six sons were slain by the king. The seventh was miraculously transferred to the womb of another wife, Vasudeva-Rohini, and was later born as Balarama. Krishna, the eighth,

---

[1] *The Bhagavad Gita,* translation and notes by S. Radhakrishnan (New York: Harper and Brothers, 1948), p. 28.

was actually born to Devaki. All the earth and heavens were filled with gladness and all sorts of portents occurred. He, wearing a yellow silk robe and bearing his customary signs, the discus, the mace, the conch, and a lotus flower, stood before them—they falling on their knees in reverence—and bade them deliver him to a cowherd mother, Yasodha, who at the same moment had borne a girl child. This they did, presenting the child of Yasodha as their own to King Kamsa, who, seeing it was but a girl, saw no reason to destroy it. Thus was Krishna's life preserved, and he lived as a child and youth in this bucolic setting, with Balarama as his constant companion.

As a child, he was a prodigy of strength. Once when he was left by his nurse lying beneath a cart, an evil being saw him and sat on the cart in order to crush it and so destroy him. Krishna, with a kick overturned the cart and killed the demon. On another occasion his mother, to prevent his wandering too far, tied a rope around his waist and fastened it to a huge wooden mortar. The young Krishna ran away with it, and as he ran, the mortar caught between two large trees. He ran on without stopping, simply uprooting the trees.

Krishna was full of fun and was always playing tricks, as a boy. He loved butter, and because he often stole some from the milkmaids, or *gopis*, they came to call him "Butterthief" and complained of him to his mother. As a boy, he also performed many miracles. Once Krishna and some of the herd boys were wandering in the forest and came upon what they thought was a mountain cave. Really, it was the open mouth of a dragon, who thus thought to destroy Krishna. As they went near to look in, the monster drew in his breath, and the boys were swept into the **dragon's** mouth. The mouth snapped shut, and the poisonous breath of the dragon threatened to destroy them. But the boy Krishna made himself bigger and bigger until the dragon's stomach burst and all of them were delivered unhurt.

As he grew older, he became a favorite of the *gopis* or milkmaids. When he played his flute in the woods, they would go out into the forest to look for him. Once, it is said, the herd-girls went to a retired spot to bathe in the cool stream. They left their clothes on the bank. It happened that Krishna was sitting in a tree near by, watching his herd. Playfully he stole their garments and climbed once again into the tree. As the girls were searching about for their clothes, one girl saw Krishna in the tree. "There he is," she called to the others, "who steals our hearts and our clothes."

As a lover he became famous, in the end becoming husband of more than 16,000 wives—probably the world's record. But of all the wives, it was Radha who was dearest to him. It is their love which has been celebrated in the *Gita Govinda*, or Indian *Song of Songs*.

Once the people were worshipping Indra, who was the Lord of Rain and King of Heaven. Krishna sought to dissuade them. Indra, angered at this opposition, sent such heavy rainstorms that the people feared destruction. They called upon Krishna, crying, "You caused us to give up the worship of Indra. Come now and protect us against his wrath." Whereupon Krishna lifted a mountain with his little finger and held it as an umbrella over them until Indra, recognizing Krishna's superior power, gave up the conflict.

The *Chandogya Upanishad* refers to Krishna Devakiputra, the son of Devaki, and speaks of him as a pupil of Ghora Angirasa, who was a priest of the sun.

In the Epic, Krishna appears again and again as a warrior —quite apart from the *Gita*, with no suggestion of any divine character. In the end he dies, shot by the enemy in his only vulnerable spot—the sole of his foot—as he sits in the forest.

How, then, does he become a God? Scholars reconstruct Krishna's history differently. One theory is that there was a clan leader in the north known as Vasudeva. He became the object of a devotional cult—some think, the sole object; that is, that he was conceived of as a monotheistic deity. The basis for this latter belief is not so certain. Other clans were attracted to this worship, and by a process of syncretism their own tribal hero Krishna, who also had remote connections with a pastoral cowherd people, became identified with Vasudeva. Eventually this composite figure became associated with the old Vedic sungod, Vishnu, and ultimately was rationalized as his *avatar* or incarnation.

Thus, while Krishna has an historical basis, it is not clear and specific but must be deduced, and never certainly, from a variety of scattered sources. Most Krishna devotees, while assuming that he is an historical figure, put no great stress upon it but are content rather with seeking meaningful personal relationship with him at the level most congenial to their own cultural status. Some concentrate mainly upon the baby Krishna. There is a substantial cult of infancy closely resembling the cult of the *Bambino* in Italian Roman Catholicism. There is also a cult of the lover Krishna, based upon the legendary tales of Krishna's amorous exploits. At the lower level, this has sometimes

appeared, to Western eyes, at least, as a highly erotic cult.
At the higher level, it has used these stories very much as
Christian mystics have used the Song of Solomon. The
love, particularly of Krishna and Radha, has served almost
as a manual for mystics who have found in that love relationship a fit language to describe their own union with
God.

Krishna rises to the highest point of development, of
course, in the *Bhagavad Gita*, which has become India's
most popular scripture, read and loved quite beyond sectarian limits. Much of what we shall say of him here is
drawn from this source, for it is at this level that he stands
on a plane where he may be compared to Jesus, the
Christ.

The *Bhagavad Gita* deserves to be universally read. It
has found a great deal of acceptance in the West. Probably more than forty different translations of it have been
made into English. It is found in the great epic of India,
the *Mahabharata*. It is clearly not part of the epic proper,
but one of the most important parts of the didactic epic,
that is, of a vast mass of material deemed of value but
only very loosely integrated with the narrative. The *Gita*
could be omitted without in any serious way affecting
the general movement in the epic.

In the prologue, the setting is given. The opposing
armies of the Kurus and the Pandavas, rival clans of the
Bharatas, are lined up ready for battle. Krishna, disguised
as the charioteer, and the warrior Arjuna, armed for com-
bat, are standing in their chariot awaiting the sound of
the conch shell which will be their signal to charge the
foe. There ensues a conversation, which runs through
eighteen chapters, between Krishna and Arjuna. And

what Krishna says here is the religious message of the book. Thought by many scholars to be a much redacted original *Upanishad*, it comes out in the end as a strongly Vishnuite document, forming the major source of the belief in Krishna as an *avatar*, or incarnation of Vishnu. In its major emphasis, it may be said to be a book of devotion, probably the best expression of the attitude in Hinduism of *Bhakti*, or the idea of salvation by faith, love, service, or devotion to God. But it is not exclusive in this respect. It also expresses the way of salvation by knowledge, *Jnana Marga*, and that of salvation by works, *Karma Marga*. This generous recognition of the three ways of salvation gives it its universal appeal. When it further opens the way, not alone to the highborn, but to those of any caste—and women, too—it speaks to *Everyman* in India. No wonder it is India's most popular scripture!

In many ways, Krishna and Christ are alike. Superficially, at their births unusual occurrences are reported. Both grew up in humble surroundings, although Krishna was of noble birth. Both performed miracles in their youth—at least, according to legendary or apocryphal sources. The New Testament gives no account of such powers. Jesus' only recorded appearance in his childhood was at the temple at the age of twelve years, when he showed a quite precocious interest in serious theological matters, as is indicated in his engaging in discussion with the elders in the temple.

At a deeper level, they are alike in that both are incarnations of God in human form. There will be found a difference of opinion among Christian scholars as to whether Jesus so regarded Himself. The answer depends on how the scriptures are thought of and whether the

Gospel of John is to be taken as a dependable original source as to what Jesus thought concerning Himself. That He thought of Himself as standing in a special relationship to God, and as sent of God with the good news of the coming of the Kingdom, there can be no doubt at all. Nor is there any doubt that orthodox Christianity believes that in the Gospels He did proclaim Himself as the incarnation of God. "I and the Father are one," "He that hath seen me hath seen the Father," and other like passages are considered evidence that He did so regard Himself.

Krishna boldly proclaims himself to be an embodiment of Vishnu. In a classic passage in the *Gita*, he states the Indian theory of incarnation very explicitly.

> When Righteousness
> Declines, O Bharata! when Wickedness
> Is strong, I rise, from age to age, and take
> Visible shape, and move a man with men,
> Succoring the good, thrusting the evil back,
> And setting Virtue on her seat again.[2]

Here is a clear doctrine of incarnation. God takes human form and moves as a man among men. So far, it fits precisely the Christian concept of the incarnation. It differs sharply, however, from the Christian belief in asserting the principle of repeated incarnations instead of one and one only, as has been consistently held by orthodox Christianity. Hinduism embraces the idea of plural incarnations. The great Vishnu has, in their belief, manifested himself in many different forms. Systematic theology has reduced the theoretical number to ten, nine of which have already appeared, leaving one yet to be ex-

---

[2] *The Song Celestial,* translated by Sir Edwin Arnold (Boston: Roberts Brothers, 1890), Chapter 4, p. 47. It appears in various editions.

pected. Probably hundreds of alleged incarnations could be found in the extensive sectarian and orthodox Hindu writings, if all who have been so considered by some smaller or larger Hindu groups were to be taken into account. The fact that theoretically there is one yet to come makes it almost inevitable that from time to time an individual will rise and announce that he is the expected one. And there will always be some who will recognize him as such. It is quite certain that there are Indians today who would accord that status to Mahatma Gandhi. Chaitanya, founder of one of the late Hindu sects, is regarded as an incarnation by his sectaries.

This theory of incarnation—plural or recurrent incarnations—fits perfectly into the framework of philosophical Hinduism which thinks of Brahman, the neuter world soul, the one alone Real, as manifesting himself—more properly, itself—first of all in personal form in the great Hindu Trimurti, Brahma, the Creator; Vishnu, the Preserver; and Shiva, the Destroyer. But even these need more concrete form; so the human incarnation, in the case of Vishnu, brings him down to needy humanity in the fashion of a man, whenever the need appears. On the basis of this theory, not a few Hindus are perfectly willing to affirm that Jesus, for whom they have the very highest regard, is the incarnation for this age, as Krishna and Rama and Buddha were for theirs. But they will not accept him as *the unique* incarnation, to the exclusion of all others, as orthodox Christianity has always claimed. A comparatively recent book by a Ramakrishna Swami, resident in America,[3] leaves no doubt that Jesus is an incarnation of God. He sounds much more orthodoxly Christian

---

[3] Swami Akhilananda, *A Hindu View of Christ* (New York: Harper and Brothers, 1946).

than some left-wing Christian theologians in this respect. But, in the end, Jesus only takes His place in the long line of successive incarnations.

Again, Jesus and Krishna are both savior divinities. For Christians, to cite evidence in the case of Jesus is surely superfluous. All too familiar is the slogan—some times painted on billboards or rocks on the hillside along the nation's highways, or emblazoned in Neon lights on some church steeple or store-front mission—"Jesus saves." "I am come to seek and to save that which was lost" is a clear word of Jesus. And practically every Christian, whether orthodox or liberal or left-wing, holds that, in some effective way, man's salvation is bound up with Jesus. The different groups of Christians do not agree upon the way —whether the way is by His life, or by His death, or by His teachings, or all together—but they do consider Him integral to the salvation process. Some would not even hold that, in a literal sense, "There is none other name under heaven given among men, whereby we must be saved." Some would believe that salvation might come through other saviors also, but certainly Jesus Himself they would think of as in some way a savior.

In the *Gita*, Krishna boldly asserts that it is in him that men find salvation.

> Who cleave, who seek in me
> Refuge from birth and death, those have the Truth.[4]

Here it may be that the definition of salvation is different from that of salvation as conceived by Christians— "refuge from birth"—but, whatever it is, it comes through Krishna as savior.

· Again:

---

[4] Arnold, *op. cit.*, Chapter 7, p. 77.

Thou too, when heart and mind are fixed on Me
Shalt surely come to Me. All who cleave
With never-wavering will of firmest faith
Owning none other gods: all come to Me.[5]

These and many other passages in the *Gita* have the ring of the Gospels.

Furthermore, both Jesus and the Krishna of the *Gita* are universal in their outlook. "Come unto me all ye who labor and are heavy laden, and I will give you rest," said Jesus. "Go ye into all the world and preach the gospel"— whether or not these are the direct words of Jesus, they certainly express the logic of His general attitude of love for all mankind. "Whosoever cometh unto me I will in no wise cast out." In this there is certainly no limitation of race or class or sex upon His forthgoing love.

Krishna expresses much the same universality of outlook in one dramatic passage in the *Gita*, where he cuts straight through the sharply drawn caste and sex lines and opens the way of salvation to all who will avail themselves of it. "Be certain," he cries,

> . . . none can perish trusting Me!
> O Pritha's Son, whoso will turn to Me,
> Though they be born from the very womb of Sin,
> Woman or man; sprung of the Vaisya caste
> Or lowly disregarded Sudra,—all
> Plant foot upon the highest path; how then
> The holy Brahmans and my Royal Saints?
> All ye who into this ill world are come—
> Fleeting and false—set your faith fast on Me,
> Fix heart and thought on Me! Adore Me! Bring
> Offerings to Me! Make Me prostrations! Make
> Me your Supremest joy! and, undivided,
> Unto my Rest your spirits shall be guided! [6]

---

[5] *Ibid.*, Chapter 8, p. 81.
[6] *Ibid.*, Chapter 9, pp. 93–94.

It is undoubtedly this generous inclusiveness which attracts people of all classes, women as well as men, to Krishna. Not only the educated, the great, the rich, the high-caste—but the lowliest, too, can find salvation in Krishna.

Again, both Jesus and Krishna call for a high degree of personal loyalty and devotion on the part of their followers. Recall with me some of the sayings of Jesus. Found probably in greater number in the Gospel of John, they are scattered through all the Gospels. "Whosoever would come after me, let him take up his cross and follow me." "Who hath not left father and mother . . . is not worthy of me." "I have not called you servants, but friends." "I am the vine, ye are the branches." "Simon, son of Jonas, lovest thou me?" Samples could be given by the dozens.

The *Gita* is full of like sayings by Krishna:

> . . . him will I swiftly lift
> Forth from life's ocean of distress and death
> Whose soul clings fast to Me. Cling thou to Me!
> Clasp Me with heart and mind! So shalt thou dwell
> Surely with Me on high.[7]

> . . . if thou cans't not worship steadfastly,
> Work for Me, toil in works pleasing to Me!
> For he that laboreth right for love of Me
> Shall finally attain, but if in this
> Thy faint heart fails, bring Me thy failure! Find
> Refuge in Me! let fruits of labor go,
> Renouncing all for Me, with lowliest heart,
> So shalt thou come.[8]

Near the end of the special chapter, the twelfth, which

---

[7] *Ibid.*, Chapter 12, p. 131.
[8] *Ibid.*, Chapter 12, p. 132.

exalts particularly "*bhakti-yoga*," he describes at length the man he loves:

> Who, seeking Me, heart and soul vowed unto Me, ...
> Who, fixed in faith in Me. . . .
> Who, linked by no ties to earth, steadfast in Me. . . .
> . . . But most of all I love
> Those happy ones to whom 'tis life to live
> The single fervid faith and love unseeing,
> Drinking the blessed *Amrit* of my Being! [9]

Love, that is, is the attitude most desired of those who look to him.

And both put strong emphasis upon righteousness. Love expresses itself precisely in those terms. "If ye love me, keep my commandments," said Jesus, and the Gospels are replete with moral demands upon those who would follow Him. Need I repeat them here?

But they are also found in the *Gita*. Whatever may be the moral judgment upon the Krishna of the *Vishnu Purana* and of popular worship which has proved shocking to Westerners in some respects, the Krishna of the *Gita* moves upon a high moral plane.

In the chapter from which I have just quoted, where Krishna describes the man he loves, I quoted for the moment only three lines expressive of personal devotion, but in the text they were linked with high moral requirements.

> . . . Who hateth naught
> Of all which lives, living himself benign,
> Compassionate, from arrogance exempt,
> Exempt from love of self, unchangeable
> By good or ill, patient, contented, firm
> In faith, mastering himself, true to his word,

[9] *Ibid.*, pp. 133–134, *passim.*

Seeking Me, heart and soul; vowed unto Me,—
That man I love! Who troubleth not his kind
And is not troubled by them; clear of wrath,
Living too high for gladness, grief, or fear,
That man I love. . . .[10]

But perhaps it is in the sixteenth chapter that Krishna
most completely sets forth his ethical ideal.

Fearlessness, singleness of soul, the will
Always to strive for wisdom; open hand
And governed appetites; and piety
And love of lonely study; humbleness,
Uprightness, heed to injure naught which lives,
Truthfulness, slowness unto wrath, a mind
That letteth go what others prize;
And equanimity, and charity
Which spieth no man's faults; and tenderness
Towards all that suffer; a contented heart
Fluttered by no desires; a bearing mild,
Modest, and grave, with manhood nobly mixed
With patience, fortitude, and purity;
An unrevengeful spirit, never given
To rate itself too high;—such be the signs
O Indian Prince! of him whose feet are set
On that fair path which leads to heavenly birth! [11]

An analysis of the passage might lead to the observa-
tion that the emphasis is rather upon the passive than
the active, but that would on the whole be true of the
general Indian outlook. But here is surely an emphasis
upon the moral aspect of religion, not the merely emotional or the intellectual. Mere devotion is not enough.
It must bear fruit in the lives of those who love if it is to
be effective in leading to man's salvation.

---

[10] *Ibid.*, pp. 132–133.
[11] *Ibid.*, pp. 156–157.

And there are other passages elsewhere in the *Gita* that emphasize a more active gospel:

> No man shall 'scape from act
> By shunning action; nay and none shall come
> By mere renouncements unto perfectness.
>
> . . . He who sits
> Suppressing all the instruments of the flesh
> Yet in his idle heart thinking on them,
> Plays the inept and guilty hypocrite. . . .
> Do thine allotted task!
> Work is more excellent than idleness;
> The body's life proceeds not, lacking work,
> There is a task of holiness to do. . . .
> . . . such earthly duty do
> Free from desire and thou shalt well perform
> Thy heavenly purpose.[12]

But if Jesus and Krishna are alike in these important aspects—and they are important—they nevertheless differ significantly at other points.

First and perhaps most significantly, they differ in respect to the incarnation. As already indicated, Krishna sets forth the doctrine of multiple incarnations, not just one. There is no hint of such an idea in the Gospels. Although there are many people who call themselves Christians in the world today who differentiate sharply between Jesus and the Christ, who regard the Christ as independent of the human Jesus, save that Jesus bodied forth the Christ for a little time in Palestine as He has also been manifested in other forms, this, it may safely be said, is not grounded in the Gospels.

Another significant difference between the two is in respect to their attitudes toward the use of violence. Now,

---

[12] *Ibid.*, Chapter 3, pp. 38–39.

there is repeated mention of *ahimsa* in the *Gita*. It appears
in some of the passages quoted above. This is quite in
keeping with Hinduism, where it has been a prominent
ethical principle from very early times. It was part of
early Buddhism which carries back to the sixth century
B.C., and it is probably much older. The Jains, who were
earlier than the Buddhists, have cherished and developed
the doctrine more than any other group.

But in the early portions of the *Gita*, Krishna the god
clearly supports the idea of killing, urging Arjuna to rid
himself of the weakness of shrinking from it, and to do
his task of killing with untroubled mind. It is interesting
that Mr. Gandhi, the modern apostle of *ahimsa*, or non-
violence, thought he found support for it in the *Gita*.
But let us look at it.

As the warrior Arjuna looked upon his foes, many of
them friends and relatives, his heart—the warrior's heart
—"melted into pity," and he said to Krishna,

> Krishna, as I behold, come here to shed
> Their common blood, yon concourse of our kin,
> My members fail, my tongue dries in my mouth,
> A shudder thrills my body, and my hair
> Bristles with horror; from my weak hand slips
> Gandiv, the goodly bow; a fever burns
> My skin to parching. . . .
> Nothing do I perceive save woe and wail.
> It is not good, O Keshav! naught of good
> Can spring from mutual slaughter! Lo, I hate
> Triumph and domination, wealth and ease,
> Thus sadly won! Alas! what victory
> Can bring delight, Govinda, what rich spoils
> Could profit; what recompense; what span
> Of life itself seem sweet, bought with such blood?
> . . . Shall I deal death on these

Even though they seek to slay us? Not one blow,
O Madhusudan! will I strike to gain
The rule of all Three Worlds; then how much less
To seize an earthly kingdom. . . .
Better I deem it, if my kinsmen strike,
To face them weaponless, and bare my breast
To shaft and spear, than answer blow for blow.[13]

Here is a noble protest against war, the noblest ever
spoken by a warrior. How did Krishna react to it? He
spoke thus to Arjuna, and, remember, it is the god speaking, and it is his word that is the authoritative teaching
of the poem.

How hath this weakness taken thee? Whence springs
The inglorious trouble, shameful to the brave,
Barring the path of virtue? Nay, Arjuna,
Forbid thyself to feebleness! It mars
Thy warrior-name. Cast off the coward-fit!
Wake. Be thyself! Arise, scourge of thy foes!

But Arjuna cried,

How can I, in the battle, shoot with shafts
On Bhisma, or on Drona. . . .
Better to live on beggar's bread
With those we love alive,
Than taste their blood in rich feasts spread
And guiltily survive.
Ah! were it worse—who knows?—to be
Victor or vanquished here. . .?
I know not what would heal the grief
Burned into soul and sense,
If I were earth's unchallenged chief—
A god—and these gone hence. . . .
And sighing, "I will not fight," held silence.

---

[13] *Ibid.*, Chapter 1, pp. 17–20, *passim.*

JESUS AND KRISHNA

Once more Krishna, the god, spoke, seeking to sway
his determination:

Thou grievest where no grief should be! Thou
    speakest
Words lacking wisdom! for the wise in heart
Mourn not for those that live, nor those that die.
Nor I, nor thou, nor any one of these
Ever was not, nor ever will not be,
Forever and forever afterwards.
All that doth live, lives always. . . .
. . . . Let them perish, Prince! and fight!
He who shall say, "Lo, I have slain a man!"
He who shall think, "Lo, I am slain!" those both
Know naught! Life cannot slay. Life is not slain.

       . . .

Who knoweth it (life) exhaustless, self-sustained,
Immortal, indestructible—shall such
Say, "I have killed a man, or caused to kill?"
    Nay, but as when one layeth
    His worn-out robes away
    And, taking new ones, sayeth,
    "These will I wear today!"
    So putteth by the spirit
    Lightly its garb of flesh.

       . . .

This Life within all living things, my Prince!
Hides beyond harm; scorn thou to suffer, then,
For that which cannot suffer. Do thy part!
Be mindful of thy name and tremble not!
Naught better can betide a martial soul
Than lawful war; happy the warrior
To whom comes joy of battle—comes as now,
Glorious and fair, unsought; opening for him
A gateway unto Heaven. But if thou shunn'st
This honorable field—a Kshatriya—
If, knowing thy duty and thy task, thou bidd'st

Duty and task go by—that shall be sin!
And those to come shall speak thee infamy
From age to age; but infamy is worse
For men of noble blood to bear than death.[14]

So spoke the god Krishna. Clearly, here is a deep difference from the teaching and practice of Jesus. Not everyone is convinced that Jesus was a complete pacifist. I happen to be one who is. I do not find any support in anything He said or did for participating in the slaughter of war. His doctrine of loving one's enemies, turning the other cheek, going the second mile—all of which He demonstrated perfectly in His own manner of life—are worlds away from the urging of Krishna that Arjuna rise and scourge his foes—that "naught better can betide a martial soul than lawful war."

Jesus and Krishna differ notably also in their concept of God. Jesus, in the full tradition of His people, thinks of God in almost wholly personal terms. God is, of course, the creator and sustainer of the universe. He is the author and guarantor of the moral order. He is the rewarder of good and evil. But God is best described in terms of love. He is the Father—not in a mere sense of progenitor, but in a moral and spiritual sense. No other term so adequately expresses His thought. He thinks of Himself— at least, in the Gospel of John, He says so—as showing forth the Father. "He that hath seen me, hath seen the Father." There is nothing complicated about it. "I am come to do the will of my Father" is one way of expressing His sense of mission. What Jesus may have thought of God in modern metaphysical terms there is no way of knowing, if, indeed, He ever troubled Himself to think

14 *Ibid.*, Chapter 2, pp. 26–28, *passim.*

in such terms. God's purpose in the world—a purpose which man could, if he willed, thwart at least in part—was to establish His Kingdom. Jesus appeared first on the scene preaching repentance and preparation for the coming of that Kingdom, precisely the message of John the Baptist. God was, for Him, one, of course. He assumes this as a matter of course, as a part of His tradition. There was no place in His thought for any other divinity. He, as a Jew, must have repeated daily the *Shema*, dear to all pious Jews, "Hear, O Israel, the Lord our God is one Lord," and one Lord only did He worship. Neoorthodox theologians castigate liberals for oversimplifying the thought of Jesus, particularly for their supposed overemphasis upon His kindliness and compassion, to the exclusion of the sternness of His judgment upon sinners. That there is a stern note even in the Gospels cannot be denied, but that it overshadows the other element can hardly be urged. In any event, this does not greatly change the essentially simple, uncomplicated character of Jesus' thought about God which we have suggested.

Krishna, in the *Gita*, stands just as much in the tradition of historic Hinduism as Jesus does in that of the Hebrews. Perhaps we oversimplify it also when we say that this thought—expressed through the *Upanishads* and the great commentators upon them—is that there is one ultimate reality which cannot be described in precise terms. When in one of the dialogues in the *Upanishads* a teacher tries to do so, he can only end with the exclamation, *"neti, neti"* —"no, no, not that." This ultimate reality is defined as the "Unseen seer, the unheard hearer, the ununderstood understander," as the "Imperishable"—all negative terms. Positive terms used are the "One Alone Real," "The

World-soul," and Brahman-Atman, and this Brahman seems to comprehend in himself all the world. Outside of Brahman there is nothing that exists. He is again and again identified with the totality of all that is. Described by some as a monistic concept, philosophically, this fits precisely the definition of pantheism in the area of religion.

Before the *Gita* appeared, Brahman the alone Real had come to be thought of as manifesting itself—one can hardly say himself, for "Brahman" is neuter—in Brahma the Creator, Vishnu the Preserver, and Shiva the Destroyer. That was the Hindu way of creating a synthesis of the various sectarian systems that had arisen. And by the time the *Gita*, which probably passed through various stages of editing, assumed its present form, it had become a Vishnuite document, with Krishna the incarnation of Vishnu. But he is more than that. He is ultimate reality itself, as can be seen in numerous passages in the Song Celestial.

Arjuna asks, "Who is that Brahma?"

Krishna replies, "I Brahma am! The One Eternal God."

Again Krishna calls himself "The One, The Invisible, The Unrevealed, Unnamed, Unthinkable, All-pervading Highest, Sure."[15]

And that he thinks of this One in monistic or pantheistic fashion is clear from Krishna's declaration that he is the very womb from which the universe was born. "Know," he cries, "Know! I am that womb."

> I make and I unmake this universe.
> Than me there is no other maker.
> . . . All these hang on me
> As hangs a row of pearls upon its string.

Thus far he might be thought of only as the effective

[15] *Ibid.*, Chapter 12, p. 130.

creator of the world, as in the Hebrew, but he goes on
to say,

> I am the fresh taste of the water; I
> The silver of the moon, the gold 'o the sun,
> The word of worship in the beds, the thrill
> That passeth in the ether, and the strength
> Of man's shed seed. I am the good sweet smell
> Of the moistened earth, I am the fire-red light,
> The vital air, moving in all which moves;
> The holiness of hallowed souls, the root
> Undying whence hath sprung whatever is;
> The wisdom of the wise, the intellect
> Of the informed, the greatness of the great,
> The splendor of the splendid.[16]

Or, once more,

> I am the Sacrifice! I am the prayer!
> I am the Funeral-cake set for the dead!
> I am the healing herb! I am the *Ghee*,
> The *Mantra* and the flame, and that which burns!
> I am—of all this boundless Universe—
> The Father, Mother, Ancestor, and Guard;
> The end of Learning! That which purifies
> In lustral water. I am One! I am
> Rig-Veda, Sama-Veda, Yajur-Ved;
> The Way, the Fosterer, the Lord, the Judge.
> ... Seed and Seed-Sower,
> Whence endless harvests spring! Sun's heat is mine,
> Heaven's rain is mine to grant or to withhold;
> Death am I, and Immortal Life I am,
> Arjuna, *Sat* and *Asat*, Visible Life
> And Life Invisible.[17]

Arjuna longed to see Krishna in all his reality and glory,

---

[16] *Ibid.*, Chapter 7, p. 73.
[17] *Ibid.*, Chapter 9, pp. 89–90.

Unable to do this with human eyes, he is given another form and permitted to gaze upon him. Krishna then says,

> Gaze then, thou Son of Pritha,
>
> . . .
>
> Behold this is the Universe! Look! what is live and dead
> I gather all in one—in Me! Gaze as thy lips have said,
> On God, Eternal, Very God! See Me! See what thou prayest! [18]

There ensues then in this Chapter Eleven a description of what Arjuna saw—one of the most eloquent and moving attempts in the whole literature of world's religions to describe the power and majesty and glory of God. Read it entire, preferably in the Edwin Arnold translation. Arjuna looked,

> . . . But sore amazed,
> Thrilled, o'erfilled, dazzled, and dazed,
> Arjuna knelt, and bowed his head,
> And clasped his palms, and cried, and said. . . .
> "Thou Brahm, than Brahma greater,
> Thou God of Gods, Life's Dwelling-Place and Rest." [19]

Surely in all this there appears a concept of God unlike, though not wholly so, the simpler one of the Man of Galilee.

There is also a clear distinction between Jesus and Krishna in respect to their belief in immortality. Jesus seems quite clearly to have taught an ongoing life, individual and personal, after the crisis of death. There is

---

[18] *Ibid.*, Chapter 11, p. 107.
[19] *Ibid.*, Chapter 11, pp. 110, 121.

no unmistakable blueprint of the exact form it takes. He
refused to give a specific picture of it. When the lawyers
came to Him with the question as to whose wife a woman
would be who had successively married, in levirate fashion, seven brothers, His answer was that in heaven there
is neither marrying nor giving in marriage. He spoke
often of eternal life, and thought of it as being a present
possibility—of everlasting life—of the moral judgment
which man must meet at the great assize, when men will
be judged not on the basis of what they have said, but of
what they have done. "For as much as ye did it unto
one of the least of these my brethren, ye have done it unto
me." In John 14 He says, "I go to prepare a place for
you—that where I am, there ye may be also."

In the *Gita*, Krishna speaks the familiar language of
Hinduism in this respect. Man is born again and again
as his *Karma* requires; but the end of all his striving is an
escape from birth. Thus he finds "the peace beyond, My
peace, the peace of High Nirvana" What the extent of
this existence is, is not told. If one fails to reach this at
one time, he is not lost. He comes at death

> Unto the Region of the Just; dwells there
> Measureless years, and being born anew,
> Beginneth life again in some fair home
> Amid the mild and happy.[20]

That is, he may be born for a time into some heaven or
hell; but, when his *Karma* warrants, he returns to birth
again. His final salvation is when he "comes to birth no
more." As to the meaning of this, in concrete terms, there
is no completely clear picture. It is called a state of supreme bliss, yet at the same time it is affirmed—though

[20] *Ibid.*, Chapter 6, pp. 65, 70.

not in the *Gita*, that I can discover—that there is no consciousness, no memory, no activity, and no individuality.
The little self has been lost in the total self of the universe.

This is quite in keeping with the general Hindu attitude
toward the individual, which is in sharp contrast with
that of the Christian.

What have their followers done with them? It is, of
course, clear that the *Gita* already represents the result of a
long process of development of the thought about Krishna.
It records the high point in that development which carried him from a probably historical figure, or perhaps
various figures, to the complete deification. Here he has
become Brahman, the ultimate reality itself.

But he has been thought of by the Bhakta primarily as
savior, and there have arisen some very interesting discus-
sions of how this comes about. Rudolf Otto's *India's Religion of Grace* [21] explores this, and in it can be found
parallels for almost all the various theories as to the work
of Christ in Christianity. Very prominently appears the
thought of Krishna's superabundant mercy, which is im-
puted through faith to the devotee.

Two schools, both believing implicitly in Krishna's
saviorhood, differ sharply as to how salvation is achieved.
What must the believer do? One says that he must do only
one thing; namely, absolutely surrender his will to Krishna.
As a kitten yields itself completely to the mother cat to
be carried by the nape of the neck whither she will, so
must the devotee yield himself wholly to Krishna. Who
does not find in this a parallel to the old gospel song,

    All to Jesus I surrender, All to him I freely give . . .

Who of the older generation has not heard in revival meet-

---

[21] London: Student Christian Movement Press, 1930.

ings and on the lips of "personal workers" phrases such as, "Just surrender," "You've nothing to do but throw yourself on the mercy of Christ."

But the other school holds that man has more of an active part in the process. This group takes as its symbol the baby monkey. How is it carried? By the mother, of course; but how? Only by clinging fast to the mother. Should it loose its hold, it would fall to the ground. That is, the process of salvation is one in which the believer has an active and a continuing part. Inertness, surrender, is not enough. This, of course, has abundant parallels within Christianity.

> Are ye able, says the Master,
> To be crucified with me. . . .
>
> Must Jesus bear the cross alone
> And all the world go free?
> No, there's a cross for everyone
> And there's a cross for me.

Of course, in the case of Krishna, there is no conception of his death as in any way efficacious, as in that of Jesus, where the death figures even more largely than His life or His teachings as the basis of the atonement. There is Pauline support for this view when he writes, "If Christ be not risen, then is your faith vain," for, of course, this presupposes His death. And many find it in Jesus' own statement that the Son of Man came to give His life a ransom for many for the remission of sins, although this does not necessarily imply His death.

One final parallel may be noted; namely, that between the expected coming of a tenth incarnation and the second coming of Jesus. That is, there is a sense of expectancy among Hindus just as there is among Christians, and not a few have identified one or another saint or sectarian founder as the expected one. But there is no strong apocalyptic sense in which the expected incarnation is awaited. The general cyclic concept which underlies Hindu thought precludes that. The world—indeed, the universe itself—will one day revert once again to the state of complete disintegration, into its component elements and inertness, in which it will remain, utterly quiescent, until once more the process of evolution begins.

So Christ and Krishna stand side by side. One suspects that, as the centuries pass and the various cultures of the world interpenetrate ever more deeply, there will be an increasing tendency for them to flow together. This will be resisted by the Christian world, for Christianity—itself in large measure, historically, a syncretism—has at any given period felt that it was unique, and that it must be kept from mingling with any lesser faith. In the process, it seems to one Christian observer, perhaps because of his own Christian background, that Krishna is far more likely to become Christ-like than Jesus to become Krishna-like. Could it be that this is the way in which the fulfillment of the prophecy in scripture is to be realized—"That every knee shall bow and every tongue confess that Jesus Christ is Lord to the glory of the Father"?

4

Jesus and Mahavira

———————□———————

AMONG THE MOST NOTABLE TEMPLES OF INDIA, THAT LAND
of temples and shrines, are those of the Jains who, strangely
enough, in theory at least, renounce all belief in any one
being or many beings, aside from man himself, upon whom
he may depend for help in his struggle to achieve what we
of the Christian world call salvation and the Jains themselves, *moksha*. Figures there are, twenty-four of them,
sometimes colossal in size, before whom worshippers may
be found prostrating themselves, or even making some kind
of an offering. But none of these is God. They are Tirthankaras, ford-finders, paragons who have found the way
across the abyss of death to birthlessness after the long
round of repeated births in human, sub-human, or even
divine form but are powerless to help anyone else on his
way. They stand as mute witnesses to the possibility that
man may achieve *moksha*, for have they not done so?

There is a rich literature of legend concerning these figures. That it is the work of a luxuriant imagination may
be seen in the enormous size attributed to them, especially
the earlier ones. The sons of the very first, Rishabhadeva,
are said to have been 500 bow-shots high. He lived an
unimaginably long time ago, and himself lived eighty-four

lakhs or eight million four hundred thousand *purva* of time.

By the time the twenty-third of the list is reached, a more historical character, Parsvanatha, emerges, so that some scholars believe that he actually lived, antedating the birth of Mahavira by some two centuries. Mahavira himself is so wrought into this legendary lore that early Western scholars decided that he, too, was only a mythical figure and not a real man. But further research has convinced most scholars that he did really live, that he was an older contemporary of Gautama, the Buddha, one whom Buddha may have followed in his early search for enlightenment, his years of ascetic practice. The exact dates of his birth and death are not known, Jaina tradition giving them as 599-527 B. C.

There is a very substantial Jain literature in which the story of Mahavira appears. The Kalpa Sutra is the one which gives most extensive information concerning the founder, although others, particularly the Acaranga Sutra, supply material concerning his life and teachings. The two major sects of the faith preserve variant traditions which, while in the main agreeing, are nevertheless at times quite contradictory. One says he never married; the other, that he did. One makes him a completely naked asectic, the other has him wearing some apparel. But in both he emerges substantially as an austere figure, extreme in his asceticism, insistent upon *ahimsa*, or non-injury, and quite independent of any help from outside powers in his quest for *moksha*. When the sources upon which we must rely for an account of the respective founders are compared, those for Jesus are the better furnished. The Gospels, while not wholly without a legendary element, present a rather clearer historical human figure than do the sacred books of the Jains; also, they are much closer in time to the period they describe—not over two generations at most. Probably the basic teachings of both are fairly well preserved in their respective scriptures.

How are these two, Jesus and Mahavira, alike—and how do they differ? First, the resemblances:

First of all, the events surrounding their birth are unusual. Those surrounding Jesus are too familiar to need repetition here, the Annunciation, the visit of Mary and Elizabeth, and so forth.

According to the Kalpa Sutra, Devananda, wife of Rishabhadatta, lying on her couch in a state between sleeping and waking, had a marvelous dream in which she saw an elephant and a bull, a lion, a lotus lake, the ocean—in all, fourteen objects. She went to her husband and told him, inquiring what it might signify. "O beloved of the gods," he replied, "we shall have a son, a handsome boy, who when grown will know all the lore of the Vedas, the Angas, Upangas, will be versed in philosophy and mathematics, and be very learned in many sciences."

The birth was in no sense virgin, for it is related that, accepting the meaning of the dream, she enjoyed together with her husband the "noble permitted pleasures of human nature." In that night was Mahavira conceived.[1]

But the chief and king of the Gods, Sakra, learning of this, hastened to worship and do reverence to the child. But having done this, he reflected that it simply doesn't happen that Arhats Baladevas, or Vasudevas, are born in low, poor, or brahmanical families. It were better, he thought, that the embryo be removed from the womb of Devananda to that of a nobler person. Whereupon he gave

---

1 *Kalpa Sutra*, translated by Max Müller, *Sacred Books of the East* (London: Oxford University Press, 1881), Vol. 22, p. 222.

an order that Mahavira be transferred to the womb of Trisala, and her unborn child be transferred to the womb of Devananda, and this was done while both were in a deep sleep on the 83rd day after conception. Trisala was of the noble warrior caste. She, like Devananda, had a wonderful dream of fourteen objects on the night the transfer was made, for every mother of a Tirthankara sees these fourteen objects in a dream when she conceives her remarkable son.

In due time—specifically, after the lapse of nine months, seven and a half days, "while all the planets were in their exaltations, the moon in her principal conjunction, and the sky in all its directions clear, bright and pure; while a favorable and agreeable low wind swept the earth, at the time when all fields were green and all people were glad and amusing themselves, she gave birth to a perfectly healthy boy." [2]

In the night when he was born, it is said that there was a divine light occasioned by many gods and goddesses ascending and descending, and that a great shower of silver, gold, diamonds, garlands, flowers, and riches rained down upon the palace of the king Siddartha, his father. He was given the name *Vardhamana*.

As in the case of Jesus, Mahavira seems to have remained at home with his parents until he reached thirty years of age. Unlike Jesus, the narrative places him in an atmosphere of extreme luxury—as a child, he had five nurses, we are told: a wet nurse, a bathing nurse, one who dressed him, one to play with him, and one who carried him about. One account states that he married and had a daughter, while still living as a prince at court.

[2] *Ibid.*, Vol. 22, p. 25.

What went on in the mind of either during these years we do not surely know. Mahavira was apparently influenced by a monastic group who had their headquarters near by in a grove, for, a year after the death of his parents, he renounced his life of privilege and luxury as a prince and became an ascetic, a monk of the order of Parshva. His initiation into this fraternity included pulling out his hair in five handfuls. He did not long remain with the order, but became for twelve years a wandering mendicant. Through austerity—going naked in cold and heat, eating only what was given him in his begging bowl, exercising the most meticulous care not to kill even an insect in his pathway—he sought the destruction of the clinging karma which was the cause of rebirth.

It was in the thirteenth year of his wandering and rigorous ascetic practice that one day, while seated in deep meditation near a sal tree on the bank of a river not far from the town of Grimbhikagrama, he reached his goal called Nirvana, and thus became a Conqueror or Jina, never to be reborn. He was now forty-two years of age. On reaching this stage, he took five vows, which are basic now to Jainism.

1. I renounce all killing of living beings.
2. I renounce all vices of lying speech arising from anger, greed, fear, or mirth.
3. I renounce all taking of anything not given.
4. I renounce all sexual pleasures, either with gods or men or animals.
5. I renounce all attachments, whether little or much, small or great, living or lifeless.[3]

This marked the beginning of a thirty years' ministry of

---

[3] *Acaranga Sutra*, Lecture 15, *ibid.*, Vol. 22, pp. 202–210.

teaching, winning disciples, and establishing the Jain brotherhood. He was a Kevalin, and eventually took his place as the twenty-fourth and last of the ford-finders who show others the way to *moksha* though they can in no way aid them directly. This experience corresponds roughly, therefore, to that of Jesus at His baptism and the subsequent temptation experience signalizing the beginning of His active public ministry.

The point of greatest similarity in the ideas of Jesus and Mahavira lies in their attitude toward killing. Both were unalterably opposed to the taking of human life, and both were at one in their teaching and practice of non-violent resistance to those who sought to do them evil. Jesus' words in the sermon on the mount are too familiar to require stressing. His doctrine of "Love your enemies— pray for them that persecute you, turn the other cheek, go the second mile" led Jesus, when reviled, to revile not again; when scourged, to seek no retaliation; "as a lamb before her shearers is dumb, so opened he not his mouth." It led Him to pray for his murderers, "Father forgive them, for they know not what they do." Jaina Sutras are full of stories of Mahavira and his calm, non-resisting endurance of pain and mistreatment at the hands of his fellows. There is the account of a group of cruel villagers who, finding the naked ascetic meditating in the countryside, lighted a fire between his feet to see if he would flinch. They are said even to have driven nails into his ears. Mahavira uttered not a word, but, as the narrative says, humbled himself and bore the pain.

> In a certain country natives attacked him, dogs bit him. The Venerable One endured it being perfectly enlightened.

He was struck with sticks, fists, lances, clods. When he once sat down they cut his body, tore his hair, threw dust upon him. They tossed him into the air and let him fall. "The Venerable One humbled himself and bore pain, free from desire." . . . Bearing all hardships, the Venerable One undisturbed proceeded on the road to Nirvana.[4]

Mahavira went far beyond Jesus in the matter of not taking life—*ahimsa*. Not only would he not take human life, but he refrained from the destruction of even the lowliest forms of life. He brushed the pathway before him in order that he might not inadvertently step on and crush any insect or worm. He strained the water he drank. He would not even kill harmful insects.

Obviously, this aversion to all killing made him a pacifist, for war cannot be fought without killing—that is, any kind but a "war without violence," such as Mahatma Gandi was to wage centuries later in India to win India's independence. Nor were his monks to engage in war. Later there arose an interpretation of his teaching which did make place for war in the life of a Jain. Laymen, because of the practical difficulty of abstaining absolutely from *himsa* or injury to life, were taught to observe the principle of *ahimsa* as far as possible. Thus I have found even the profession of soldier included in the list of activities in which a Jain layman might lawfully engage, although traditionally Jains have not usually entered miltary service. I doubt if this could be justified on the basis of anything Mahavira himself taught or practiced. It is interesting that, in recent years, a Jain revival is taking place in India—and one feature of it is a new magazine named *The Voice of*

---

[4] *Acaranga Sutra, ibid.*, Vol. 22, p. 85.

Ahimsa, which is said to be the basis of the world peace for which humanity so eagerly yearns.

Like Jesus, Mahavira gave utterance to the Golden Rule, characteristically stated in the negative, however, extending it specifically to cover all creatures. It is stated thus:

> "In happiness and suffering, in joy and grief, we should regard all creatures as we regard our own self, and should refrain from afflicting upon others such injury as would appear undesirable to us if inflicted upon ourselves." (Yogasastra) [5]

Both Jesus and Mahavira have a profoundly ethical outlook. There is a moral order in the universe. Indeed, Jainism, since it makes no place for God, is often called an ethical philosophy rather than a religion. In Jainism, as in Christianity, retribution is a constant factor. The Christian, to use Paul's word, not Jesus', believes that whatsoever a man soweth, that shall he also reap. Jesus implies it in his saying, "Do men gather figs of thistles?" In Jainism, as taught by Mahavira, it is Karma, or the accumulation of the results of one's evil deeds, which keeps him on the wheel of birth. To escape birth, one must rid himself of Karma, which is represented graphically as something that sticks to one and builds up layer after layer as he continues to commit evil deeds. One must find a means to cleanse himself of this before he can attain *moksha*—or be saved.

That is to say, both Jesus and Mahavira hold that salvation is no mere forensic matter. It is ethically conditioned. Some Christian interpreters will declare that there is more to it than this, that there is a theological requirement as well, and certainly that is the current belief for many Christian churches. There are statements in the Gospels

---

[5] *Sayings of Lord Mahavira,* ed. by K. P. Jain, p. 6.

which indicate that Jesus may not have felt that way about it. In the great judgment scene in Matthew 25, it is difficult to find any theological test which is applied to those who stand in the great assize upon which their entrance into the Kingdom is to be based. It rather seems to be a matter of feeding the hungry, visiting the sick, clothing the naked, caring for those in prison, giving the thirsty to drink that counts. "Inasmuch as ye did it unto one of the least of these my brethren, ye did it unto me."

Both Jesus and Mahavira believe in at least the possibility of ultimate salvation for every man. So far as I can discover, it is rather in Paul that the doctrine of election first appears. Jesus opens the door wide to whomsoever will come after him. This does not guarantee that everyone will be saved—for man is endowed with freedom of will and may choose whether he will or will not pay the price of entrance into the Kingdom of God. Likewise, Mahavira. Salvation is at a price—and a high one, but not beyond the reach of any man. He may not achieve it in one life or many, but rebirth continues and there seems always to exist the possibility that he will be able to rid himself of the Karma which keeps him on the wheel.

How do the two figures differ? Already we have noted that one lived in luxury, the other in relative poverty before beginning his mission; that one had a very long ministry and the other a very short one; that one married and the other did not. And one died a natural death at a ripe old age while the other died young on a cross, crucified by his enemies.

In respect to their ideas, the basic difference lies in their world view. Jesus, as we have so often said, believed profoundly in God, and, not alone as an ethical being, the support of the moral order, but as a loving Father by whom He had been sent to call men to fellowship with Himself in the Kingdom of heaven. Mahavira, while not disbelieving in God or the gods, of whom he spoke frequently, made no place in his system for dependence upon any. If there were superior beings—a fact which he seemed to recognize—they were still finite beings and subject, just as humans were, to the round of rebirth. Yet modern Jains do not like to be called atheists. And, in the long course of their development, they have come to regard the ford-finders essentially as divinities, praying before them and bringing offerings to them—at least at the popular level—in very much the same way that Hindus and other religionists do. Technically, the worship is of a subjective nature only, as was noted in connection with Buddhism.[6] Man is helped only as he contemplates what these figures have been able to do. He knows thus that he can achieve *moksha* and is thereby encouraged.

A further fundamental difference follows naturally from this difference of world view. Since there is no one on whom man may depend for help toward his goal of release from rebirth, he is dependent solely upon himself. Once a follower came to Mahavira and asked what help he might discover in his quest for release. "Man, thou art thine own friend," Mahavira replied. "Why wishest thou for a friend beyond thyself?"[7] This, of course, is sheer humanism, and it is owing to this fact that many will not recognize Jainism as a religion at all. At least, they would relegate it to the disputed classification of humanistic religion. It is certainly not theistic.

---

[6] See p. 40.
[7] *Acaranga Sutra*, Müller, *op. cit.*, Vol. 22, p. 33.

As to what man may and must do to attain to birthless-ness, Mahavira and his followers are quite explicit. There are the three jewels, right knowledge, right thought, and right conduct, which run rather parallel to at least a part of Buddha's Eightfold Path. These are defined in very great detail. In the end, two major requirements are set forth as the *sine qua non* of salvation: these are the practice of *ahimsa*—non-injury, or non-killing—and asceticism. These clearly put his system in the classification of salvation by works—not by knowledge or by faith. One earns salvation by his own unaided effort through the practice of austerity and the faithful observance of ahimsa. All these requirements are spelled out in the vows which even a layman must take. There is, so far as I can see, no element of grace, which plays so signal a role in the Christian idea of salvation.

We need not here repeat that Christianity as taught by Jesus is not ascetic, or that it did not require complete renunciation of the world. This came later, as a phase of developing Christianity, but can hardly be based upon the teachings of Jesus as they appear in the Gospels. Asceticism seems to be an extraneous growth upon the Christian faith which delayed some centuries in appearing. It is, on the other hand, the very heart of Jainism.

Since there is no God against whom man has sinned, there is no place for repentance and forgiveness of sin, which are so prominent in Jesus' teaching. "Repent ye, for the Kingdom of God is at hand" was central in Jesus' preaching.

Salvation, in the case of Mahavira, is defined primarily in terms of birthlessness. When this has been achieved, what then? There is little or no positive content provided us for the term in Jainism, any more than in Hinduism. There are proximate heavens and hells, borrowed from Hinduism, into which men may be born for a season in the round of transmigration; but they are, in the nature of the case, transitory and impermanent, for out of them man must come eventually to take up the weary round of birth.

Nor does Jesus ever give a blueprint of what lies beyond this life. In John he says, "I go to prepare a place for you, that where I am, there ye may be also." But wherever and whatever it is, personal fellowship with God in his Kingdom seems an integral part of it.

No great theological structure has been built around Mahavira. He has been venerated. The marvelous stories and legends that have been woven about him lift him high above the ordinary human—and, it may be, tend to deify him. But never so at the verbal level. They never pray to him, since, lacking any God to whom prayer can be directed, prayer seems useless—that is, in any other than a purely subjective sense. I may contemplate Mahavira along with the other twenty-three Tirthankaras, and may derive encouragement from the belief that they have trod the long, hard road ahead of me and managed to reach birthlessness, thus proving that it can be done—but that is all. There can certainly never be a prayer of petition to an outside objective being, for, by very definition, there is none.

It is true that a doctrine of the sinlessness of Mahavira has arisen, as in the case of Jesus. The Acaranga Sutra says of him: "Having wisdom, Mahavira committed no sin himself nor did he induce others to do so, nor did he consent to the sin of others." But a little farther on, he was still called an erring mortal, "He meditated free from sin

and desire, not attached to sounds or colors; though still
an erring mortal, he wandered about and never acted care-
lessly."[8] And in the Kalpa Sutra, omniscience—which is
ordinarily an attribute of divinity, not man—is attributed
to him. It declares: "He was a Kevalin, omniscient, and
comprehending all objects; he knew all conditions of the
world of gods, men, and demons, whence they came and
where they go. . . ."[9]

Mahavira is, of course, extolled as the great ascetic, an
exemplar to be emulated in the rigor of his austerity. He
is, of course, venerated as the founder of the faith, and
made the last of the twenty-four Tirthankaras, the ford-
finders who point the way to *moksha* and stand as a perpetual source of courage and hope to those who are on
the way. The ignorant and the weak may pray to him for
help, and treat him in quite the way that divinities are regarded in other faiths—but the instructed do not do so, nor
may they—for he is beyond all reach of prayer. His is the
peace and the silence and the perpetual inactivity of Nirvana. It is not strange, therefore, that there has been little
or no development of doctrine concerning his person beyond that already indicated. In the modern literature of
propaganda designed to revive the faith and set it once
again upon a world mission, Mahavira himself, save as
founder and teacher, plays little part. Among numerous
tracts and pamphlets and books, it is his teaching and his
practice, not his person, that are proclaimed. Knowing
this, man must unaided make it his own if he would attain
in the end the same deliverance which Mahavira, last of the
Tirthankaras, has also won.

---

[8] *Acaranga Sutra*, Müller, *op. cit.*, Vol. 22, p. 86.
[9] *Kalpa Sutra*, Book 2, Lecture 15:26, *ibid.*, Vol. 22, p. 201.

5

Jesus and Nanak

---------□---------

LATEST BORN OF THE GREAT FOUNDERS OF RELIGION WAS
Nanak, who founded the Sikh faith. He was a contemporary of Martin Luther, born in 1470, and died in 1540 A.
D. The faith he founded was the fourth of the world religions to take form in India. It is small in comparison with
the other great ethnic faiths, and has no appreciable following outside of India itself. All told, it numbers only about
six million followers—less than some of the larger Christian
denominations in the United States. On the basis of numbers, the Bahai faith, for an example, might with equal
right be considered one of the great religions, and on the
basis of its world-wide spread, much more so, for the Sikh
faith has made no effort to propagate itself outside of India
and is to be found, apart from India, only where Sikhs have
gone as immigrants. I recall seeing a Sikh temple, for example, in Singapore. Yet the Sikh faith is customarily
rated as one of the eleven world religions. Actually, some
regard it as only one of many Hindu reform movements,
one variant of the rather amorphous religious faith of India
which we call Hinduism. But the Sikhs themselves will
not have it so. They have always insisted in dissociating
themselves from Hinduism, in the Indian Census, as a
separate and distinct faith.

JESUS AND NANAK

Since many people have little or no idea of who the Sikhs are, let me say simply that they are the result, in organized form, of the fusion of aspects of the Hindu and Moslem faiths which occurred after the Moslem invasion of India. It has in it elements of both religions, yet it is a new synthesis of those elements which is neither Hindu nor Moslem now. This, it may be said, is the way Christianity came into being as an organized system of worship, thought, and life: it is a blending of Hebrew, Greek and Roman elements, with some things added from other cultures which it has touched in its world-wide spread.

The Sikh faith takes over Islamic monotheism, but with distinct Hindu overtones. It is decidedly non-idolatrous, and it has had about it something of the Moslem militancy which made it a once powerful Indian state. But there is in it much of Hindu *bhakti*, or devotion, and Hindu mysticism. No longer a state, there is still among the Sikhs a strong party which urges Sikh nationalism and would seek a further partition of India and the setting up of a Sikh state as well as Hindu and Moslem states.

Nanak was the founder of this modern Indian faith. What was he like—what did he teach? How was he like Jesus, and how did he and Jesus differ? How have his later followers thought of him?

Since we are much closer in time to Nanak than to any of the other founders, the sources which tell of his life and the movement that he started are more abundant than for the others. The Sikh scriptures, known as the Granth, tell very little about him factually, for they consist almost entirely of songs and poems and aphorisms not only of Nanak himself, but of several of the other successor Gurus, and a number of other poets, including the

– 87 –

great Kabir, who significantly influenced the Sikh founder. But if the scripture which is called the Adi-Granth contributes little of a factual nature, it does contain a great number of songs and poems written by Nanak which clearly set forth his ideas and reveal his general outlook and spirit. One writer, Macauliffe, has translated the whole and, instead of presenting merely the translation in order as found in the original, has attempted to provide the appropriate setting for the songs, providing thus a kind of running story of his life and activity as well as his sayings. But this, it should be said, is one man's reconstruction of the life, which may or may not be entirely correct in every detail. It is certainly from his songs that we shall attempt to set forth his ideas and religious attitudes.

In addition, there are biographies from a fairly early time which attempt to tell the story of his life, but that they contain a good deal that is legendary must now be admitted. And, of course, there is a considerable mass of legendary lore about him which circulates among the people. None of this is canonical, however.

The Granth is almost worshipped at the golden temple at Amritsar, headquarters of the Movement. All day long, every day, it rests on a dais in the temple, covered with rich brocaded silks, and thousands of Sikhs honor it. I saw considerable quantities of money—mostly coins—which had been left before it on the floor. At night it is carried across the causeway from the temple, in the middle of a lagoon, to the shore, where it is locked in a great safe. In the morning, it is carried again to the temple and properly draped with its coverings. It is the central object of the temple. Upstairs in another room sits a man reading aloud from the sacred text. He is replaced at intervals by another, and this reading goes on day and night throughout the entire day—all the year through. It is thus constantly being read, from the first page to the last, consecutively, year after year. How long this has gone on I do not know, but there is an endowment, I was told, to perpetuate the reading indefinitely.

That there is a firm historical basis for Nanak as founder of the movement there can be no doubt, although where fact ends and legend begins is not always clear.

On the basis of these sources, how are Jesus and Nanak alike, and how do they differ?

Although Nanak has been claimed by both Moslems and Hindus, the overwhelming evidence points to predominantly Hindu ancestry, and to the fact that he, like Jesus, came of humble origin. He was born near Lahore, in the Punjab, in a village later known as Rayapur, in 1469 or 1470.

Both in Islam and in Hinduism, there was a belief that there was one to come, somewhat as the Jews believed in a Messiah. In the case of the Shiah Moslems, it was a belief in an Imam, who had disappeared and would one day return again. In the case of the Hindus, there was the belief in an *avatar*, or incarnation of Vishnu, who was yet to come. It was easy for later Sikhs to see in these prophecies of one to come a foreshadowing of the coming of their leader Nanak, just as Moslems today attempt to fit Mohammed into Biblical prophecies.

His birth was attended by unusual portents. Strange sounds were heard. The midwife recognized an unusual quality in the child's voice. A great company of ascetics, holy men, and "devas," to the number of three hundred and thirty million, came to pay him honor and to witness that "a great saint had come to save the world." An astrologer, called to prepare the child's horoscope, worshipped him and predicted that he would be worshipped by both Hindus and Moslems, and would himself worship but one God. This is reminiscent of the case of Simeon at the presentation of Jesus in the temple, and of the holy man Asita who came a long distance to see the newborn Buddha and sang of his future greatness. Just as Asita wept because he would not himself live to see the great things he prophesied that the Buddha would do, so the astrologer expressed regret that he would not himself live to see his prophecies fulfilled.

The child was, as in Buddha's case, very precocious. At five years of age, he began to talk of profound religious subjects. At seven he amazed his teachers by making an acrostic based upon the alphabet.

He was educated after the manner of his day for one of his class, and thus came to know something of the scriptures of both Hinduism and Islam. When at nine years of age he went through the initiation into the "twice born," and was invested with the sacred thread, legend has it that he grasped it in his hand and uttered this verse:

> Make mercy thy cotton, contentment the twisted
> thread, and continence the knot.
> And thus make a "thread" for thy soul . . .
> A man dies, the thread is broken and his spirit
> departs without it . . .
> By praise and adoration of the Name comes honor
> and the true "thread"
> Which does not break, but lingers for man's entrance
> into the court of God.[1]

---

[1] J. C. Archer, *The Sikhs in Relation to Hindus, Moslems, Christians, and Ahmadiyyas* (Princeton, N. J.: Princeton University Press, 1946), p. 70.

He was not much interested in school. He was given to seeking solitude and meditation. He associated with *sadhus* and learned a great deal from them. He is said to have studied Persian, the language in which most of the Moslem literature was available.

His parents were troubled about him and his future. They wondered if he were not mad. They got him employment as a herdsman, but he was not watchful of his herds, and they trampled the fields of the neighbors. Naturally, the neighbors were angry with him. But here, as frequently in the legendary lore about him, a miracle came to his rescue, and the fields were completely restored. On another day, while out with his flock, he fell asleep beneath the shade of a tree. It was observed that, strangely enough, the shade of the tree remained stationary in order to protect him as he slept, regardless of the progress of the sun. A tree still standing is pointed out today as the one under which this occurred, a great gnarled *jal* tree. On still another occasion, a poisonous cobra once spread its hood to protect him.[2]

Later he was employed as a farmer and as a shopkeeper, but he gave everything away to the holy men. His father was so exasperated by his irresponsibility that he once struck him. But Nanak was not fitted for a life of work in commerce. He loved most to be in meditation, and to sing songs of praise to God. One day, when he was alone in the forest, a vision came to him which was probably his real call. God, he thought, spoke to him, saying: "I am with thee, I have made thee happy and also all who shall take thy name. Go and repeat it, and cause others to do

---

[2] M. A. Macauliffe, *The Sikh Religion* (Oxford: Clarendon Press, 1909), Vol. I, pp. 22–29.

likewise. Abide uncontaminated by the world. Practice the repetition of my name, charity, ablutions, worship, and meditation. I have given thee this cup of nectar, a pledge of my regard."

On completing a song which is preserved in the opening section of the *Japji*, or Book of Psalms, by Nanak, a voice was heard not unlike that reported as heard by Jesus after his baptism.

"O Nanak, to him upon whom my look of kindness resteth, be thou merciful, as I too shall be merciful. My name is God, the primal Brahm, and thou are the divine Guru." [3]

He had gone into the forest with his faithful follower, Mardana, who was wont to accompany him in his songs on a musical instrument, the *rebek*. A searching party found him, and, thinking he was mad, a Moslem Mullah sought to exorcise the demon. But Nanak assured them that he was not insane, and bade Mardana play as he sang:

> Simpleton Nanak hath become mad upon the Lord
> And knoweth none other than God . . .
> When man loveth the Lord and deemeth himself worthless
> And the rest of the world good, he is called mad—[4]

It was perhaps at this time that he gave utterance to a strange saying which puzzled his hearers: "There is no Hindu; there is no Mussalman." When asked what he meant by this, he said in effect that there were only brethren under God. When asked what it meant to be a Moslem or Mussalman, he sang:

---

[3] *Ibid.*, p. 35.
[4] *Ibid.*, p. 37

To be a Mussalman is difficult . . .
Let him heartily obey the will of God, worship the
Creation and efface himself.
When he is kind to all men, then shall he be indeed
a Mussalman.

And, he went on at great length:

Make kindness thy mosque, sincerity thy prayer
carpet, what is just and lawful thy Quran . . .
Make right conduct thy Kaaba, truth thy spiritual
guide,
Good works thy creed and thy prayer . . .
If thou make good works the creed thou repeatest,
thou shall be a good Mussalman. . . . [5]

He likewise taught Hindus. Going on a journey, he
wore a costume which was a mixture of Hindu and Moslem
articles of wear. Urged by Hindus to become a Yogi,
he said:

Religion consisteth not in a patched coat, or in a
Yogi's staff or in ashes smeared over the body.
Religion consisteth not in earrings worn on a shaven
head, or in the blowing of horns.
Abide pure amid the impurities of the world; thus
shalt thou find the way of religion.
Religion consisteth not in mere words;
He who looketh on all men as equal is religious.
Religion consisteth not in wandering to tombs, or
places of cremation; or sitting in attitudes of con-
templation, . . .
Abide pure amid the impurities of the world; thus
shalt thou find the way of religion.[6]

Like Jesus, Nanak underwent a temptation experience.
Kaliyuga, or Satan, came to tempt him. Mardana was
afraid. Said Nanak:

5 *Ibid.*, p. 38.
6 *Ibid.*, p. 61.

Put the fear of God into thy heart: then the fear
of *death* shall depart in fear.[7]

Kaliyuga offered him all the world's wealth if he would
renounce his mission—a palace of pearls, inlaid with gems
—beautiful women—the power of miracles—and the
sovereignty of the East and West.

He replied that he had given up all sovereignty, and
what could he do with all Satan offered, which really
belonged to others? Satan fell at his feet and worshipped
him.[8]

There was also another temptation experience, although
on a lower physical plane. In a certain village, a band of
beautiful women under the leadership of Nur Shah—
skilled dancers and entertainers—employed all their skill
and charm on Nanak, but without success. He only
countered with songs. Then Nur Shah used every allur-
ing gesture and tempting display of her rather unusual
charms, but without avail. He only sang her a hymn.
Finally she too gave up, and all the women sought his
blessing and gave him their loyal allegiance.[9]

As in the case of Jesus, Nanak performed an itinerant
ministry. The wanderings attributed to him in the *janam
sakhis*, which are a mixture of fact and legend, take him
over much of India, visiting many of the sacred places of
pilgrimage—Benares, Puri, and others—beyond India to
Ceylon, and even as a pilgrim to Mecca, the sacred city of
Islam. Always he was accompanied by the faithful Mardana and frequently by other disciples. Once he was en-
slaved and put to heavy labor when captured by a Moslem
invader. It was noted, however, that the burden which the

[7] *Ibid.*, p. 78.
[8] *Ibid.*, p. 80.
[9] *Ibid.*, pp. 84–85.

Guru Nanak was forced to carry was raised a cubit above his head without any apparent support. When he was ordered to grind grain in a mill, it was seen to revolve of its own accord without any effort on his part. Impressed by these miracles, the Emperor released him and his followers to continue their journey. Again and again throughout the story of his life, miracles were reported as occurring— just as in the case of Jesus.

On one occasion, Mardana and he found themselves in a desert. Mardana was consumed with thirst. Said Nanak, "Eat of the fruit of yon tree." He did so and enjoyed it so much that he carried some along for the journey. But when he ate of it, he fell down, for it was poisonous. Nanak had blest it for the occasion and made it palatable. Nanak put his foot on Mardana's head, and Mardana recovered at once.[10]

Not many years before his death, he ceased his wanderings and went home to determine his successor. Passing over his own sons, one of whom had been a follower, he chose Angad, one of his disciples. He settled at Kartarpur and there ended his days. At the every end, he sat in the open, under an acacia tree whose leaves had withered but which became green again and put forth blossoms when he sat down under it. There he yielded up his life while his disciples round about him sang at his bidding. He pulled a sheet up over himself, and it is reported that there was a soft glow of light beneath the sheet. This spread and seemed to blend with a halo which formed about the head of Angad, his successor as Guru.

When next day the sheet was lifted, the place where Nanak's body had lain was empty, but on each side of it flowers bloomed. Some had wanted to bury his body;

10 *Ibid.*, pp. 94–95. He cures a leper, p. 107.

others, to burn it on a funeral pyre. The flowers were divided, and some were burned while the others were buried, thus satisfying both parties. Later both a shrine and a tomb were built, but a flood of the river Ravi washed both away. Some said that this happened so there might be no place where idol or ancestral worship might grow up about the Guru.

Jesus and Nanak are alike in that both believed in the Oneness of God. The *Mool Mantra*, the opening sentences of the *Japji*, or Psalms of Nanak, proclaim this:

> There is one God.
> He is the supreme truth.
> He, the Creator,
> Is without fear and without hate.
> He, the Omnipresent,
> Pervades the Universe.
> He is not born
> Nor does he die to be born again.
> By this grace shall thou worship him.[11]

It is reiterated again and again. He is the "True one," the "formless One"; He is Lord. He is Truth.

And although there are occasional sayings that might be interpreted as reflecting the idea of God as impersonal, or as a kind of pantheistic world soul, such as the Hindu Brahman, the overwhelming emphasis is upon God as personal. He is "the Creator," "the Giver," "the Truth". He is "Lord"; "His works are legion." Even when conceived of as "formless," he is addressed as personal, thus: "Mayst thou endure, O formless One." [12] And God is good, he is the author of all virtue. Infinite is his loving kindness. "To those who crave and seek he gives, gives with full aban-

---

[11] Kushwant Singh, translator, *The Sikhs*. By permission of The Macmillan Company, 1953, and George Allen & Unwin, Ltd., 1953.
[12] *Ibid.*, Ps. 17, 18, 19, last line.

don." [13] This is somewhat reminiscent of Jesus saying: "To him that asketh shall be given."

And it is by God's grace, ultimately, that man achieves salvation. While works are important and man is urged to cleanse himself and do good, in the end, "Salvation comes to those whose thoughts rest on the Name"—that is, God. "Their faces glow," says Nanak, "and they have become immortal." [14]

In general, Nanak seems to advocate the way of faith or devotion—*bhakti marga*—as the preferred way of salvation. "Devotion leads to happiness," saith Nanak; "Sin and sorrow are destroyed by hearkening." This is repeated as a refrain at the end of Psalms 8, 9, 10 and 11. Nanak seems definitely to have been influenced in this idea by the preachers of Hindu *bhakti*, of whom there were many in his time. Not only in Nanak, but in the writings of the other Gurus and poets included in the Adi Granth, the element of grace is emphasized. Loehlin says that the word *parshad*, which may be translated "grace," appears over six hundred times in the Adi Granth; and if other words of similar connotation were counted, the total would be well over a thousand. In the Hebrew New Testament, "grace" appears specifically 169 times. This conception of the love of God, expressing itself in acts of grace toward his peoples, is "one of the central points at which the *bhakti* and evangelical traditions come close together." [15] This grace is thought of among the Sikhs, he says, as coupled with the Guru (teacher), that is, as being mediated through him.

Nevertheless, Archer thinks that, while *bhakti marga* is

---

[13] Archer, *op. cit.*, Ps. 4, p. 121.
[14] *Ibid.*, p. 133. Last lines of postlude to the *Japji*.
[15] C. H. Loehlin, *The Sikhs and Their Book* (Lucknow: Lucknow Publishing House, 1946), p. 53.

the true way if pursued in the true Name, Nanak proposed, even though not deliberately, a fourth way—beyond works, knowledge and faith, "more instrumental and effective than any one or all of the other three", that is, the way of truth.[16] In John, Jesus is reported as saying, "You shall know the truth and the truth shall make you free."

Both Jesus and Nanak were given to frequent periods of communion with God, although neither retired permanently from the active work of the world nor recommended it.

Both were impatient with ritual requirement when it was exalted to a place of primacy. Neither penance nor pilgrimage nor even free-will giving gains merit for one unless the heart be loving, declared Nanak.[17]

> Cooking places of gold, vessels of gold,
> Lines of silver far extended,
> Ganges water, firewood of the Karauta tree,
> Eating rice boiled in milk—
> O my soul, these things are of no account
> Until thou art saturated with the true Name.[18]

He looked upon Hindu fasting and other ascetic practices as "works of darkness."

He defined a holy man as one in whom are found friendship, sympathy, pleasure at the welfare of others, and dislike of evil company.

To another he said that envy, pride, slander, and obstinacy belong to the perverse. It is necessary to relinquish these as a tree sheds its leaves in autumn.[19]

---

[16] *Ibid.*, p. 133.
[17] Archer, *op. cit.*, Ps. 21, p. 126.
[18] Macauliffe, *op. cit.*, p. 133.
[19] *Ibid.*, pp. 137, 138.

There is no merit in speech or silence; none in begging or in giving alms.

"He bestows the virtue in whose hand the power lies," which is God. That is, salvation is not won; it is a gift, by the grace of God.[20]

Jesus and Nanak were alike in that their message was for no special class or people. "Come unto me *all* ye that labor and are heavy laden," said Jesus. Nanak, in the midst of a people where rigid caste distinctions separated men and raised formidable bars to fellowship across class lines, paid no attention to such lines, and welcomed men of every class into the company of his followers. It is possible that Mardana, the musician who always accompanied him, was of the outcaste group. A *zamindar* was once offended because Nanak would eat in a low-caste home and yet refused an invitation to a feast in his honor in his own high-caste home. Nanak is said to have taken a morsel of food from the *zamindar* and one from his low-caste host and squeezed them. Out of that of Lalu, the low-caste man's, oozed milk. Out of that of the *zamindar*, blood dropped, a sign, of course, of the exploitation it represented.[21] Sikhs have not always been true to the teaching of their Gurus, but caste has not been the problem among the Sikhs that it has been in Hinduism generally.

In these ways Jesus and Nanak are alike. How do they differ? While they believe in the oneness and the moral nature of God, and that he is personal, there are, as already indicated, overtones of pantheism in the teaching of Nanak. Possibly it is only an assertion of a more highly

---

[20] Archer, *op. cit.*, Ps. 33, p. 131.
[21] *Ibid.*, p. 83.

immanentist conception than that entertained by Jesus. Coming out of the Hindu background, as Nanak did, rather than that of a Hebrew monotheism, his thought would quite naturally exhibit this feature. Moslem Sufism may also have made its contribution here. That Jesus thought of God as intimately related to man and nature is indicated in such sayings as "Consider the lilies of the field," "No sparrow that falls to the ground but God knows of it," "The very hairs of your head are numbered," and "How much more will he clothe you, O ye of little faith?" But the Christian God seems always to be outside of nature and man, over against them, controlling them, loving them, caring for them, effecting his purposes through them. Nanak is willing even to call God by the names employed among Hindus and Moslems—Brahman, Hari, Rama, even Allah, provided, says Archer, "that those who call upon him by any of these, affirm that God is not only any one of them, but indeed also more than all of them in one." [22]

There is also in Nanak's conception of God something of the arbitrariness of the Moslem Allah.

> In the end he willeth what to him is pleasing.
> He is ever Lord of Lords, saith Nanak of his rule.[23]

The translations vary, and sometimes the difference is theologically very important. It is Khushwant Singh, himself of Sikh background, who translates Psalm 2 of the *Japji* thus:

> By Him are all forms created,
> By Him infused with life and blessed,
> By Him are some to excellence elated,

[22] *Ibid.*, p. 116.
[23] *Ibid.*, *Japji*, Ps. 27, p. 129.

Others born lowly and depressed.
By His writ some have pleasure, others pain;
By His grace some are saved,
Others doomed to die, re-live, and die again.
His will encompasseth all, there be none beside.
Oh Nanak, He who knows, hath no ego and no
pride.[24]

This, if it is the correct translation, is a clear-cut doctrine of election which is to be found paralleled in Paul but not in Jesus. Archer renders it thus:

Life has come by his will, through which comes life's
exaltation.
High and low are his will, and joy and sorrow his
pleasure.
In his will alone is he blessed who runs the round of
his nature.[25]

Nanak shares with Hinduism his belief in the round of rebirth, and the idea that salvation, as in Hinduism, lies in escape from this rebirth. The old Hindu principle of Karma, or the law of the deed, is for him also that which keeps men on the wheel of birth. Although Jesus may say, "By their fruits ye shall know them," and does insist upon retribution for those who deliberately choose the evil way, there is no continuing round of birth.

As to what is meant by salvation ultimately, Nanak looked for the absorption of individual being into the being of God. This was a part of his Hindu heritage. A passage from the Granth describes it thus:

As water blends with water, when
Two streams their waves unite
The light of human life doth blend
With God's celestial light.

24 Khushwant Singh, *op. cit.*, p. 189.
25 *Ibid.*, p. 120.

> No transmigration then awaits
> The weary human soul.
> It hath attained its resting-place,
> Its peaceful crowning goal.[26]

Jesus speaks often in the Gospels of heaven and hell; little is said of these by Nanak. In the Granth as a whole, there are occasional references to hell. In one passage, it says:

> How can man be saved without the name? . . .
> Without God's name he shall not be saved. He shall die and go to hell.[27]

But in the context of Hinduism this is not eternal; rather, it is a stage in the transmigration of the soul, out of which it may be reborn, to continue its round of birth. There is a mention of a kind of Sikh heaven, called *Sach Khand*, which is promised to the blest. Learned Sikhs have sought to identify this with Nirvana. But again, in Hinduism, heaven is not a permanent resting place. It may be significant that at least three books on the Sikhs do not even include the words *heaven* and *hell* in their indices.

It is true that Jesus does not give any detail as to what he means by heaven. He does say once that there is neither marrying nor giving in marriage there. He further says, "In my father's house are many mansions," but it has been left for Christians of a later time to give content to it, one expression of which, "joy in the presence of the Lord," may not be so far from the Sikh ideal. The essential difference is the apparent continuity of individual existence in Jesus' thought, as over against the loss of individuality in the being of God, as held, apparently, by Nanak.

---

[26] Quoted by Macauliffe, *op. cit.*, p. lxv.
[27] *Ibid.*, p. 149.

While in the case of both Jesus and Nanak salvation is, or may be, by faith or devotion, both regard good works as an evidence of that devotion. Nanak makes high moral demands upon his followers thus:

> Make honesty thy steed, truth thy saddle, continence thine equestrian armour,
> The five virtues (contentment, compassion, piety, patience, morality) thine arrows and faith thy sword and shield.
> Pious men who have truth in their hearts shall obtain honor in God's court.[28]

In other superficial ways also they differ. Nanak was married and had a family. Nanak's ministry stretched over many years, in contrast to the short period of Jesus' active public life. Jesus was accompanied on his preaching tours by a group of disciples; Nanak, usually only by Mardana, who played the *rebek* or lute, and one other at times. Nanak was a poet and composed numerous songs. Jesus may have had the heart of a poet, but he wrote no verse.

Nanak apparently never thought of himself as other than a human figure, a poet, a teacher, a leader of men. It is usually held, at least by Orthodox Christians, that Jesus regarded himself as divine.

And, of course, in the manner of their respective deaths, they differ. We have already recounted that of Nanak, and the story of Jesus' death is so familiar that it does not require repetition.

There remains the question as to what his later followers have done to his memory. How have they regarded Nanak?

Well, for one thing, his birthplace is a place of pil-

---

[28] *Ibid.*, p. 127.

grimage. At first pilgramages were made usually only on the founder's birthday, in celebration of that event; but in later times, pilgrims came at any time, and now large numbers do homage at the shrine in the place of his birth.

He was thought to stand in a peculiar relation to God, as the Guru who brought salvation to men.

Probably Gur Das, scribe of Arjun, the fifth Guru, expressed the belief of the Sikhs when he wrote:

> Truth stood idly by, the while unwanted, as brahmin priests and Muslim Mullahs clashed—
> And there was no salvation for the world.
> God heard the plaint of virtue and despatched the guru Nanak to the rescue of the world . . .
> He offered to this darkest age salvation by means of worship of the one True Name.
> Nanak came indeed to give this age salvation.[29]

A Rajah, to whom a shopkeeper had declared that he had seen a great being and secured salavation, asked, "Is there one in this age who can confer salvation?" The shopkeeper replied, "Such a person is Guru Nanak. The mere repetition of his name can confer salvation." [30]

Whatever else Nanak may have been, he chose a successor to himself as Guru, or spiritual leader of his followers. This man, Angad, was not of his own family line, although eventually the succession did become hereditary. That is, there was a succession of living Gurus, through the tenth Guru, Gobind Singh. After that, the Adi Granth became the Guru, although human leaders— but not Gurus—headed the developing community. Eventually there came to be a sort of doctrine respecting the Guruship. Gobind Singh, the tenth Guru, himself enunciated the doctrine thus:

---

[29] Archer, *op. cit.*, p. 147.
[30] Macauliffe, *op. cit.*, p. 147.

He (Nanak) established religion in the Kal age,
And showed the way unto all holy men . . .
Nanak assumed the body of Angad,
And made his religion current in the world.
Afterwards Nanak was called Amar Das
As one lamp is lit from another.

He goes on to recount how:

The holy Nanak was revered as Angad
Angad was recognized as Amar Das
And Amar Das became Ram Das
The pious saw this, but not the fools,
Who thought them all distinct;
But some rare person recognized that they were all
one.[31]

Archer even speaks of the essence of guruship. Thus,
he writes:

Every faithful Sikh shared in what came to be
established as the essence of the Guruship from
Nanak through the line to Gobind Singh, then by
transposition to the Granth and finally with yet more
spiritual precision in the Akal Sat Nam.[32]

Guru Gobind Singh, tenth Guru, has only one couplet
in the Granth Sahib. It was sent to his father, Teg Bahadur,
just before the latter's martyrdom.

Strength is thine: thy fetters are loosed; thou hast
every resource.
Nanak, everything is in thy power; it is only thou
who canst assist thyself.

Is he here addressing his father as Nanak? Is he asserting
that all the Gurus are one—that they are all Nanak? In

---

[31] Dorothy Field, *The Religion of the Sikhs* (London: John Murray,
1914), from *The Wonderful Drama*, out of the Granth of Gobind Singh.
[32] Archer, *op. cit.*, p. 282.

the light of his saying in *The Wonderful Drama*,[33] this would seem to be a fair inference.

There have been those who have deified Nanak.

Archer mentions [34] that Guru Das, Arjun's scribe, in a famous poem, widely used but ultimately denied a place in the Granth, refers to Nanak as an incarnation of Vishnu. Archer asks if it might not be this fact, in part, which accounted for the exclusion of the poem from the Granth.

A modern Sikh writer in a recent book on Sikhism [35] has a section on "The Divinity of the Guru," and poses the question, "Was Nanak a divine being or a human being?" According to his discussion, there seem to be three points of view. One group, the Nirmalas, the most Hindu of the sects, regard Nanak as divine; another group regards him as an enlightened human leader; the third think of him as a perfect man who came to help others attain to perfection. This latter bears some resemblance to the Boddhisattva idea in Mahayana Buddhism.

Certainly many orthodox Sikhs who do not ascribe divinity to Nanak in so many words do ascribe to him qualities and powers which are ascribed to Jesus, whom orthodox Christians regard as divine. One finds an occasional prayer addressed to him and other Gurus.

A famous Sikh prayer, Sri Wahguru, repeated in the morning and evening after the reading or chanting of the Granth Sahib, contains this:

> Meditate on Guru Nanak
> Then on Guru Angad, Amar Das and Ram Das;
> May they assist us—

---

[33] Field, *op. cit.*, p. 109.
[34] Archer, *op. cit.*, p. 146.
[35] Sher Singh, *The Philosophy of Sikhism* (Lahore: Giyani Sikh University Press, 1944), pp. 30ff.

on through the other Gurus, then:

> Ye holy Gurus, everywhere assist us.
> May the tenth Guru . . . everywhere assist us.
> Standing in His presence, Nanak, make supplication.

The prayer ends:

> Through Nanak, may thy name, O God, be exalted
> And all prosper by thy Grace . . .[36]

What the future may do with Nanak, none can say certainly. There is a strong present trend in the Sikh community to sink back once again with Hinduism. Khushwant Singh, from whose book we have already quoted, declares as the final sentence in his book:

"If the present pace of amalgamation continues, there is little doubt that before the century has run its course Sikh religion will have become a branch of Hinduism and the Sikhs a part of the Hindu social system."[37]

Should this trend continue, it would not be surprising if Nanak would come to be thought of as only an *avatar* of Vishnu, just as have other sect founders, such, for example, as Chaitainya.

---

[36] Quoted in Field, *op. cit.*, pp. 113–114.
[37] *Ibid.*, p. 185.

6

Jesus and Confucius

────────────■────────────

THERE ARE THOSE AMONG THE CHINESE WHO WOULD OBJECT to comparing Confucius and Jesus as founders of great religions, because they say Confucianism simply is not a religion. Particularly among the literati Confucianism is a humanistic ethical system lacking in those elements which are usually associated with religion. When, for example, an effort was being made to make Confucianism the state religion in the early days of the Chinese Republic, Chinese scholars opposed the attempt on the precise ground that it was not a religion. Confucius was great because he had "made history, developed literature, promoted scholarship and equal social classes . . . but he was not a religious founder."[1] Again, "the doctrines of Confucius are not the words of a religionist."

On the other hand, others did regard it as a religion, asserting that it was a faith based on a Mandate from Heaven which Confucius felt he had received. These asserted that Confucius sacrificed to Spirits as if they were present, that he prayed, and that he felt himself under a divine mission to do what he did. And, in addition, cer-

[1] Quoted in Wing-tsit Chan, *Religious Trends in Modern China* (New York: Columbia University Press, 1953), p. 14.

tainly temples were built for sacrifice to him. Do not these facts show that it was a religion, or had aspects of religion? Yet Wing-tsit Chan says, "To this day the Chinese are practically unanimous in denying Confucianism as religion."[2]

But the western world has been unanimous—or almost so—in regarding Confucianism as a religion and Confucius as a founder of religion. Certainly it has taken the place of a religion for millions of Chinese and has exercised an influence upon them comparable to that which the great religions have had upon their respective cultures. And time has treated Confucius very much as it has the others whom everybody regards as founders of great faiths.

Very much the same kind of stories have grown up about his birth and childhood that one finds in the case of Jesus, Buddha, and others, although somewhat less extravagant.

A very old story recounts how when Confucius' young mother went to a sacred mountain to pray for a son, the leaves on the shrubs and trees stood respectfully erect, and when she left prostrated themselves before her.[3] Shortly before the birth of the child, there appeared before her an animal with one horn carrying a tablet of jade in its mouth, on which was graven a message prophecying the greatness that her son would attain. Seventy years later, just before death claimed the sage, the animal was seen to return again.

Two benevolent dragons and the five planets warded off evil influences at the time of Confucius' birth. His mother heard mysterious music, while a voice from heaven announced the birth of her son. And after his birth, the

---

[2] *Ibid.*, p. 16.
[3] Carl Crow, *Master Kung* (New York: Harper and Brothers, 1937), p. 45.

phrase "established the world by law" was found written on the breast of the newborn babe.[4]

The known facts concerning his birth are few. His father had had born to him a succession of nine daughters and but one crippled son. He finally, at the age of about 70, married a young girl of about 15, and of this union Confucius was born. Later tradition makes him a descendant of a royal family. The facts seem to be that he was of a good family, but a much impoverished one. His father died when his son was but two years old, and the child was reared by his widowed mother.

Legend, based probably upon fact, has it that he was born with a marked protuberance upon his skull, where ordinarily there is a concavity. This was regarded by later tradition as a special mark of distinction. He is reported to have been nine feet six inches tall, but the unit of measurement is not accurately known. It is probable that he was a tall man, well above the stature of most of his contemporaries. This was a natural inheritance from his father, known as Kung the tall.

Ssu-ma Ch'ien, in the *Historical Records*, one of the earliest biographies of the sage, declares, "Shuliang Ho was father of Confucius by an extra-marital union with a girl of the Yeu family." The term translated "extra-marital" here by Lin Yutang is literally "wild union," or "wilds union," which the translator thinks probably means a union in the wilds, but others think means simply that, because of the extreme age differences of the parties, was not in accord with normal procedures.

Of his childhood and youth little is known. Mother and son were obliged to live frugally. He seems to have at-

---

[4] *Ibid.*

tended school until he was about fifteen. As a small child, seeing so much of the court ritual, he is said to have become very much interested in such things and with his playmates was often to be found imitating them, sometimes carrying out the burial of an imaginary dignitary or performing some of the formal sacrifices. Known in adult life as a stickler for ritual and ceremony, it was natural that such stories should be told of his childhood.

His first job was that of keeping the granary accounts of one of the baronial houses of his native state. From this he was advanced to the more difficult task of caring for the herds raised on the public lands of the baron he served. Both of these positions were in the nature of tax-gatherers' jobs and were not such as to endear him to those with whom he must deal. He seems to have been efficient and thorough in executing his tasks, but he found no satisfaction in them.

When he was nineteen years of age, his marriage was arranged, according to the current custom of his people, with a girl from the state of Sung, from which his ancestors had come. Little is known of the marriage except that a son and two daughters were born of the union, and that eventually it was unsuccessful. Some traditions have it that there was a divorce, but this is not certain. One thing is certain: that the wife played only a very minor role in the life of the sage. The son seems not to have shared his father's interests and never achieved even modest fame as a scholar, although often enough urged by his father to become one.

His mother died shortly after the birth of the son, and he spent the alloted 27 months in mourning for her. This necessitated giving up his position. He never returned to it. He seems to have employed his leisure in study, thus laying the foundation of his later career of scholarship and teaching. Where did he study? Tradition asserts that he made a journey to the imperial capital, Loyang, and there had access to the royal archives and the opportunity to study the rituals and ceremonials of the court, as well as the collections of art and music in the great museum. It is reported that he met while there the noted mystic, then an aged man, Lao-tzu, who was to be the founder of China's other native faith, Taoism. One cannot be sure that the reported conversation between them was what was actually said, but the assertion that neither understood the other is a good example of understatement, so very different were their outlook and interest.

He became a teacher and attracted a substantial number of students or disciples. At one time he is said to have had as many as three thousand. He is believed to have held the post of Minister of Crime in his own state of Lu for a short time. The legend has it that he was so efficient in his execution of his responsibilities that crime practically disappeared in his state. But he resigned from this position because he got little support from his Duke, whose favorable attention had been withdrawn from Confucius and his successful administration by a gift of race horses and beautiful women sent him by a rival prince.

He aspired to political preferment, believing that in his principles lay the secret of a successful and happy state. But no one would give him an opportunity to put his ideas into effect, although he wandered from one state to another —honored sometimes, feted, and shown every mark of hospitality. Finally he returned, after 14 years, to his native Lu, where he apparently engaged in editorial activity and further study until death claimed him—rather a disappointed old man—at about the age of seventy.

Such seems to be the outline of his life story, as it can be reconstructed from the many legends and historic sources that have survived. It is not always possible to separate fact from legend, and scholars are in considerable disagreement as to their trustworthiness.

Actually, the sources for a life of Confucius are mostly late ones. Only one of the Chinese Classics is generally believed to have been written by him, and there is not a little reason to suppose that the work attributed to him, *The Spring and Autumn,* is a different book from the one that Confucius himself wrote. But even if *The Spring and Autumn* is regarded as genuine in its present form, it tells nothing about Confucius, for it never mentions him personally; and, being almost entirely a rather detailed and utterly colorless catalogue of events which occurred in the State of Lu over a period of years, it reveals little concerning its compiler's character.

Most valuable of the sources is the *Analects,* a collection of the reported sayings of Confucius and some of his disciples—more often than not, statements made in reply to questions his students directed to him. In some respects, it is a kind of gospel. Certainly it is the nearest thing to the Christian Gospels that we possess. Unlike the Gospels, it tells comparatively little of what he did, nor does it give much information concerning the circumstances in which a given utterance occurred. Thus, the sayings are relatively unrelated and not in context, in the way Jesus' sayings usually are found. Older Chinese scholars were more inclined than are those of more recent years to regard the book as genuinely Confucian. Some of the modern scholars credit very little of it as a trustworthy report of what he said.

Arthur Waley, for example, thinks that we are justified in supposing that the book contains few authentic sayings and that it may possibly contain none at all.[5] This goes beyond the opinion of most critical scholars. But, despite all that may be said about it, H. G. Creel is inclined to agree with most scholars that it still remains the best single source we have.[6] But he points out that the book is no-where mentioned before the beginning of the Han dynasty, and parts of it he regards as quite late. It even contains, he thinks, some definitely anti-Confucian material. Some of it has to do with Confucius' disciples rather than Confucius himself. But, in general, Creel regards it, in its main sections, as a fairly early book. The evidence pointing to this is the fact that for the most part he is a very human figure and quite understandable—not as in later legend. In it there is no claim, as in later books, that Confucius held any exalted governmental posts. He is represented, of course, as a man of conviction and strength, but he has also at times his doubts and weaknesses.

Mencius, writing more than one hundred years after Confucius, affords us some information concerning him and his thought. Mencius was Confucian in his general outlook—so much so that his books have come to be regarded as among the nine books which might be called Confucian Scriptures, although they have never been thought of as in any sense the result of divine inspiration.

The book of *Historical Records*, from about a century

[5] Arthur Waley, *The Analects of Confucius* (London: George Allen and Unwin, 1938), p. 25.

[6] See H. G. Creel, *Confucius, the Man and the Myth* (New York: The John Day Company, 1949), Appendix.

before the Christian era, contains the first attempt at a biography of Confucius, by Ssu-ma Ch'ien. Lin Yutang, in his *Wisdom of Confucius*, uses it rather uncritically, but other writers are highly critical of it and are disposed to think of it as "confused and disordered." Obviously, the writer of it was not discriminating in his use of current materials. The result is not historically a very satisfying story of Confucius' life.

The *Tso Chuan*, a commentary on *The Spring and Autumn*, gives or purports to tell the history of Lu in Confucius' own time, but it contains little concerning Confucius himself. It differs substantially from other stories told of the sage. It runs to the weird and supernatural at times.

There are, of course, numerous later books, but they were written so long after Confucius' time that they add nothing authentic to his story. To sum up the matter, the present writer's impression is that at best we have only a very fragmentary, imperfectly complete story of Confucius and his teachings, considerably less in the aggregate than we possess concerning Jesus and his teachings.

This is rather interesting, for while, so far as I know, the fact of an historic Confucius has nowhere been seriously doubted, there have been some who have attempted to show that Jesus was only a figment of the human imagination, a figure created to give an historic and concrete foundation for the ancient vegetation myth of the dying and rising god.

When everything that can be definitely regarded as only legendary in the story of Confucius has been eliminated, a few facts do remain. He was certainly a person whose major preoccupation was political science or the art of government, and at various periods of his life he occupied some administrative posts in government. He was never given the opportunity to put his theories into practice as he wished, but his teachings are more concerned with this political interest than with any other single matter.

He was undoubtedly a sage and a scholar, very deeply interested in antiquity. He is reported to have said, "I love the old things." Whether or not he may be credited with all the books attributed to him, there can be little doubt that he was greatly interested in past history. He finds in certain paragons of virtue in antiquity the models for behavior in his own generation, and in others the examples of what one ought to shun.

He was a stickler for propriety—for doing the appropriate thing at the right time and in the right place. Ceremony and ritual he profoundly believed in and thought to be of the utmost importance. It may well be doubted whether the so-called *Book of Rites* is, as we have it, the work of his hands; but that it fits in in general with Confucius' interest there can be little doubt. It may be true, as Waley declares, that Chapter X, which is taken to be a description of the personal qualities of Confucius, is merely a passage from a later book of ritual, but it seems highly probable that it is not untrue to the general character of the sage—that of a precise, methodical, extremely orderly person who demanded the same kind of propriety in others. The declaration, "If his mat was not straight, he would not sit upon it," seems too artless to be simply fabricated, if there had been no basis in fact for it.

That he was a great teacher who at one time or another had a very substantial number of pupils who followed and sought to learn from him is certain. He may never have had the total enrollment sometimes attributed to him. His instruction may often have been, and probably was, of the "Mark Hopkins on one end of a log and the student on the other" sort. But he was none the less a teacher.

That he edited and passed on to later generations a great deal of material that was current in his day, leaving upon it in so doing the impress of his own personality, may be accepted as true. Certainly he may not have edited all that is now ascribed to him, but some of it he almost certainly did. It is thought that it was in this work that he spent the later years of his life, after his return from seeking the opportunity to put his political principles into effect in a practical way.

His reported preoccupation with the *Book of Changes*, if it may be depended upon as true, indicates that he was deeply interested in what we would today call the occult, for this book is essentially one of divination. It has always seemed to me to be rather contrary to the ordinary down-to-earth, common-sense character of Confucius to accept as true his reported utterance to the effect that, if he had another fifty years to live, he would dedicate all of it to the study of the *Book of Changes*.

The tradition of his interest in music is a strong one and is probably based upon fact. He seems to have been a great lover of music and to have found deep satisfaction in it.

That he died a disappointed man—owing to the unwillingness of those in authority to take seriously his political theories is quite clear.

And, finally, it is quite certain that he was a profoundly religious man, although religion was never a major concern. This will be disputed by some writers, who find in his expressed unwillingness to speculate concerning the gods, or the afterlife, an indication of his essential humanistic, or non-theistic, view of the world. But one may be profoundly religious and still not wish to enter into speculation concerning religion, believing that, after all, it is a matter of faith rather than reason, and that no good will result from seeking to prove it. Of course, specific sayings of Confucious are often called into question, and those expressive of a profound conviction concerning Heaven as ordering the world, and as demanding or causing this or that, may be attributed to later writers who have read these ideas back into Confucious' own utterances, but it seems to me to be doubtful. That they may have read more into his words than he intended may very well be, but that they have completely distorted an otherwise wholly non-theistic outlook is more difficult to believe. If such an outlook is not specifically that of Confucius, it certainly is of the Confucianism of the *Doctrine of the Mean*, where there is a definitely religious note.

There are some interesting similarities and differences in the careers of Jesus and Confucius. Jesus lived only into His early thirties; Confucius rounded out his three-score years and ten. Jesus' ministry was not over three years—possibly, considerably less. Confucius had a long career—perhaps some forty years of active teaching or governing or of literary pursuits.

Jesus, while probably the support of the family after Joseph's death, never married. Confucius did marry, had children, and knew the responsibilities of a householder.

Both were teachers *par excellence*. Both were peripathetic, wandering over a more or less extended area.

Both had an inner group of disciples. Jesus often taught the multitudes; Confucius, apparently only his pupils. Jesus used the story method most commonly, perhaps because He did speak so much in informal fashion to simple, unlearned people. Confucius seldom did this, and his instruction was probably more formal, given chiefly to students of serious purpose. Both were masters of epigrammatic utterance. Both knew well how to turn a phrase, how to put much into few words. "Blessed are the pure in heart, for they shall see God," said Jesus. "No man can serve two masters"; "He that loseth his life shall find it."

Confucius said: "The superior man blames himself; the inferior man blames others." "The superior man is ashamed that his words are better than his deeds." "It is man that makes truth great, and not truth that makes man great." "Don't criticize others' faults; criticize your own."

Confucius died as an old man. He fell ill, and a disciple came to visit him. The Master, asking why he had come so late, sang, "The great mountain crumbles; the roof beam is breaking; the wise man is passing away." Grieving, the disciple cried, "If the great mountain crumbles, to what shall I look up; if the strong beam gives way, what will protect me? If the wise man passes away, on whom shall I lean?"

Confucius then is said to have wept and told the disciple of a dream he had had which seemed to him to portend his own death. "For a long time," he cried, "the world has been unregulated, and no ruler has been able to follow me." Seven days later, in 479 B. C., the sage died at the age of 73.

Jesus, as every Christian knows, died as a young man in all the vigor of young manhood, crucified upon a cross, praying, "Father, forgive them, for they know not what they do."

For one, it was the end. For the other, at least as believed by His followers, based upon many reported utterances of Jesus, it was not the end at all. As told in the probably late Gospel of John, He had said, "It is expedient for you that I go away, but if I go I will send the Comforter and he shall guide you into all truth."

Certainly Jesus seems to have shrunk from death, as recorded in His prayer in the garden, "Father, if it be thy will, let this cup pass from me," and on the cross, "My God, My God, why hast thou forsaken me?" But He had also said in the garden, "Nevertheless, not my will, but Thine be done." Once more shaken on the cross to cry out in despair, He nevertheless died with a prayer of resignation upon His lips, "Father, into thy hand I commend my spirit."

But at the deeper levels of belief and outlook on the world, how do they compare? First, in what do they agree —for points of agreement are always more important than points of difference?

First of all, they were, I think, in fundamental agreement in the belief in the moral order of the universe. Certainly this is true on the basis of works attributed to Confucius. We are here in something of a dilemma. Scholars seem to think that the number of sayings which may surely be attributed to him are few. But they do not agree among themselves as to precisely which ones these are. How, then, is one to deal with them, and to know just what the original Confucius said? For that matter, the same is true in the case of Jesus. Shall one take only the residue after individual scholars have rejected one after another of the things they said? But, very obviously, this would not be quite fair. Often scholarly judgments are influenced by subjective considerations, so that one cannot affirm positively that they represent the truth.

What we are interested in here is not so much to compare Jesus and Confucius or the others as they really were —for that we can never know completely. Rather, it is our purpose to compare the Jesus and Confucius and Buddha, and so on, who appear in the canonical scriptures which developed around their persons and their teachings, for this, once it has been established, is what exercises its continuing influence upon the passing centuries. To be sure, the Confucius as he really was influenced people during his own lifetime by what he really was and what he really did. These entertained certain ideas concerning him and his teachings which they passed on to the next generation, which in turn passed them on as they apprehended them to the next generation. Finally, these ideas and attitudes found expression in written form which became the officially received, authoritative basis for men's understanding of the man and his teachings. Even if these have changed materially in the process, they are what have exercised whatever continuing influence the founder and his teachings have had upon his culture.

Jesus may or may not have been the person set forth in the Gospel of John. Indeed, as seen in contrast with the simple, straightforward story told by Mark, he does not seem to have been. But it has been the Christ of John's Gospel who has most deeply affected the Christian world. And it has been the Confucius represented in the canonical books who has left his imprint upon Chinese culture.

Confucius may never have edited the *Book of History*

or the *Odes*—but China has thought so for 2000 years and drunk deeply at the fountain of his supposed editorial genius. The *Doctrine of the Mean* and the *Great Learning* may not be from his hands, but they have represented Confucius to the Chinese for twenty centuries.

In the *Book of History* there is clear recognition of the moral nature of the universe. Again and again, he refers to the retribution Heaven has sent down upon evil rulers. More than once, a given ruler is represented as acting as an instrument of Heaven in the execution of Heaven's judgments. Heaven sends down calamities upon those who act insolently and do evil, he declares. Heaven bestows its rewards on the virtuous but condemns the guilty, for whom various punishments are prescribed.[7] It is Heaven's way to bless the good and make the evil ones miserable.[8]

The *Doctrine of the Mean* is rather generally attributed to a grandson of Confucius, and it is not certainly known that Confucius believed all that is set forth in the book. It is quite possible that it is more profoundly religious in its outlook than Confucius really was. It calls the ordinances of God the law of our being, declares that when true moral being and moral order are realized, the universe becomes truly a cosmos. It declares further that there is no place in earth or heaven where the moral law does not reign: it is supreme over heaven and earth. It represents Confucius as saying that the moral laws form one system with the laws by which Heaven and earth support and contain all things—and that it is the one system running through everything that makes the Universe so impressively great.[9]

---

[7] *Shu King*, Part II, Book III.

[8] *Sacred Books of the East* (London: Oxford University Press, 1881), Vol. 3, p. 90.

[9] *The Conduct of Life*, Wisdom of the East Series (London: John Murray 1920), pp. 31–53, *passim*.

That Jesus held to this same view is too familiar a fact to require repeating here, although He regarded God, the author of the moral law of the Universe, as a much more personal power than did Confucius—but of that, more later. Confucius is probably closer to the Old Testament view than he is to the New Testament in some respects.

They were in agreement also in the belief in the principle of reciprocity as a guide to moral behavior. Jesus puts it in the familiar "Do unto others as you would that men should do unto you"—the Golden Rule.

Confucius more often put it in the negative form, sometimes called the Silver Rule: "What I would not have others do to me, I do not do unto them" [10] or "never do unto others what you would not like them to do to you." [11] "When one carries out the principles of conscientousness and reciprocity, he is not far from the moral law," [12] he said. He humbly recognized that in his own behavior he had not been able to carry it out perfectly, but it was none the less the ideal. In stating this, he gave it the positive form. Said he: "To serve my father as I would expect my son to serve me, that I have not been able to do. To serve my sovereign as I would expect a minister under me to serve me, that I have not been able to do." So also in his behavior toward elder brothers and friends, he had not been able to do what he would have desired of them.

In my next statement of fundamental agreement, I do not feel that I stand on such sure ground. I am sure some will disagree with me. It is in the matter of their doctrine of human nature. Was it inherently good, neutral, or

---

[10] *Analects*, Book XII, 2, Waley, *op. cit.*
[11] *Analects*, Book XV, 23, translated by James Legge, *Sacred Books of the East*, *op. cit.*
[12] *Doctrine of the Mean*, Book XIII, 3–4.

bad? Unfortunately, neither can be held to have stated the matter unequivocally. And later expounders of the respective faiths have not been in entire agreement. The weight of later Christian tradition—notably its doctrine of original sin—has thrown doubt upon the idea that Jesus thought of human nature as inherently good. To be sure, man was originally created good; but with the fall in the Garden, sin entered and left an entail of sinfulness upon all the children of father Adam. Paul certainly held this; but did Jesus? To be sure, Jesus recognized the sinfulness of men and their need of repentance. But that could well be the case even if man were born inherently inclined toward the good, for actually men are affected by their environment, in which admittedly sin is a constantly present factor. Even the inherently good are free to choose the evil and, if they do so, stand in need of redemption. I am not able to put my finger upon any precise saying of Jesus which categorically states a doctrine of human nature; but, as I read his words, it seems to me that I find nothing that declares that it is evil. It seems rather to be either neutral or good. In his characterization of man as a child of God—a son and heir—he seems to me to be putting the weight of his thinking on the side of man's essential goodness. For is not God good? Confucius is clearer in his statement than Jesus, and among many of his followers, the idea of man's inherent goodness was insisted upon. One tried to say that human nature was neutral, like water which would flow indifferently toward the East or the West. To which a witty Confucian scholar retorted, "Yes, it will flow east or west, but it will not flow freely upward or downward." It was, he thought, the nature of man to move toward the good as it was the nature of water to flow downhill.

Again, they were in agreement in stressing the centrality of family relationships as the essential pattern of ideal moral behavior. Jesus makes the Fatherhood of God a central feature of his faith, and man's relationships with other men dependent upon their common sonship of the Father God. And this Father-Son relationship is thought of, not simply in terms of progenitorship, but rather in moral terms. Confucius makes the Father-Son relationship the most important and demanding of all human relationships. Filial piety or devotion is the cornerstone of Confucian ethics. Doubtless there are serious differences in the practical way in which this is worked out in concrete human behavior, but there does seem to be a fundamental agreement at bottom. This, too, will probably be questioned by some who read.

With agreement on all these rather important points, they differ very widely at others. In the first place, Confucius' whole teaching is fundamentally this-wordly in character. To be sure, he believed in an ongoing life. His own earnest practice and commendation of the practice of ancestor worship is an evidence of this. But he had little to say of the life beyond this one. God rewarded good and punished evil, but in this present life, not in heaven or hell. Jesus as represented in the Gospels, unquestionably believed in and emphasized life after death, and in future rewards and punishment, although He was by no means indifferent to what happens here and now. Jesus' whole teaching was God-centered. Everything else in His system flows form this basic fact. Man is not alone in the universe. God creates and sustains the universe and man, and man's salvation depends not wholly upon man himself.

Confucius, as we have seen, undoubtedly believed in Heaven or God, but much of his teaching was given without any reference to God. It was distinctly humanistic in its general emphasis, although not wholly so.

Jesus thought of God in very personal terms. God is not merely creator: He is Father, and He is concerned for His creatures. His very nature is love. God is love. So much did He love men that He took the initiative in seeking man and sending His own Son to bring him to repentance and salvation.

Confucius, on the other hand, thought of God in relatively impersonal terms. Heaven, which is an impersonal way of speaking about God, ordains this or that, sends down good or evil, but there is little or nothing of warmth in God's relationship with man. As a natural result, while Christianity develops as a religion of devotion, Confucianism is, if a religion at all, one of duty.

A very deep difference between Jesus and Confucius is that vicarious suffering is central in Jesus but totally lacking in Confucius. Jesus seemed to think of His own death as somehow necessary in order that man might be redeemed. One need not accept all the extreme statements of the theologians as to the nature of Christ's work in order to realize that Jesus saw His own death as in some sense redemptive, something suffered, not for any evil He had wrought, but vicariously in order that man might thereby be brought into right relationship with God—or be saved. Jesus seems almost literally to have accepted as the pattern of His own life the description of the suffering servant of Isaiah 53: "He was bruised for our iniquities. The chastisement of our peace was upon him, and by his stripes are we healed."

On the side of ethics, Confucianism has no Sermon on the Mount, and Jesus' radical statements concerning turning the other cheek, going the second mile, and loving one's enemies, Confucius would by no means have accepted. When it was reported to him that his older contemporary Lao-tzu had spoken of overcoming evil with good, he enunciated the principle which has been basic to Confucian ethics ever since. Said Confucius, "Requite good with good, but evil with Justice," and in this he probably has vastly more followers, even among Christians, than Jesus has, really, for His revolutionary principle of requiting enmity with love. Thus, a Chinese pacifist would find no theoretical support for his position in Confucius' teaching.

Even so, Confucius had a great horror of war and a low estimate of the military. Once asked about government, Confucius said, "Peoples must have sufficient to eat; there must be a sufficient army; and there must be confidence of the people in the ruler." To which his questioner asked, "If you were forced to give up one of these . . . which would you go without first?" Confucius answered: "I would go without the army first." The confidence of the people in the ruler he regarded as most basic of the three— even above that of sufficiency of food—for if the confidence in the ruler were there, food should be forthcoming. Some who think that Lao-tzu was earlier than Confucius wonder if this may not represent some influence of Lao-tzu upon the sage.

We of the West are familar enough with the way in which Christianity came to regard Jesus. He became a member of the Holy Trinity—very God of very God, according to the Athanasian creed, although not all Christians have held so high a Christology. Minority groups resisted the tendency to His deification in the early centuries and since, the modern Unitarians and others in the more liberal churches representing that resistance in our modern world. But how have Confucius' followers come to think of him with the passing centuries?

Confucius was, first of all, of course, reverenced as an ancestor by his own family. In that there was nothing extraordinary. But gradually, as his influence grew, he came to be reverenced by others as well. What may well be called his gradual apotheosis began formally in the year 1 A. D., when he was canonized as Duke Ni, the all Complete and all Illustrious. Fifty-six years later, orders were promulgated requiring sacrifices to be offered to him in all Colleges. In the year 89 A. D., he was raised to the rank of Earl; and in 267 A. D. more elaborate sacrifices, including that of animals, were ordered celebrated four times each year. More than two hundred years later—in 491— he was officially canonized as the Venerable Ni, the Accomplished Sage. Separate temples for him were decreed in the capitals of the various provinces in 555 A. D., and in 740 A. D. his image was moved to the central place in the Imperial College. The year 1067 A. D. saw him raised to the full rank of Emperor, and in 1907 his full apotheosis was attained when he was raised by the Dowager Empress of China to full rank with the deities of Heaven and Earth. Just what underlay his successive promotions to higher rank is not known in every case. But it is well known now that the final advancement by the head of the Manchu dynasty was a sop to the Chinese literati in an attempt to hold their loyalty in the face of the revolution which was already impending and which broke soon afterward, carrying down that imperial dynasty.

But, with all this, there has never developed any significant theological doctrine around his person. Even with the sacrifices made to him, the approach—at least of the intelligentsia, who have mainly kept alive his cult—was never that of seeking his aid in the attainment of salvation. Prayers there were, to be sure, but they were prayers rather expressive of reverence and veneration than those of petition. Through him was sought no propitiation for sin, or forgiveness. They were, rather, honorific and eulogistic, and even expressive of gratitude. Indeed, many Chinese deny that they pray to him at all, but say rather that they honor him as we do our great who have passed on; that they make a sacrifice to him, very much in the same spirit as we place a wreath at Washington's or Lincoln's tomb. Insofar as the illiterate worshippers are concerned—although it is chiefly the literate who have frequented his temples—it is probable that they thought of him very much as they did of the other gods.

Confucius is universally ranked as sage among the Chinese, however else he may be thought of by them. His influence has been chiefly that of a teacher, and it has been perpetuated primarily through the educational system. Chinese ethics are largely Confucian ethics, although tempered in some degree by both Taoism and Buddhism. His influence upon the political life through the requirement that those aspiring to political preferment must pass rigorous examinations on the classics is well known. But this passed with the coming of the revolution. A strong effort was made to have Confucianism adopted as the State religion, but this failed. This statute would have carried with it compulsory instruction in Confucian philosophy and ethics in the schools and colleges, but that proposal also failed. The result has been a gradual lessening of Confucian learning and influence. The coming of Communism threatens its destruction, for the Communists are making every effort to counteract it and destroy it. They know that so long as the idea of filial devotion survives, they can never wholly command the unquestioning loyalty of Chinese to the Communist State. Who will win out in the struggle, no one knows. But, as it has been aptly observed, Chinese culture is an anvil that has worn out many hammers. I personally believe that it will outwear Communism —not every phase of it, of course, but a great deal of it will.

In conclusion, Confucius looked, in general, to the past. For him, the golden age lay there. "I love the ancient things," he cried, and he was never happier than in the study of the past. The great paragons of virtue were there, and he was always looking back across the years to them.

Jesus, too, had a regard for the past. "I came not to destroy the law," he declared. But the Kingdom of God, for him, lay not in the past. He viewed the past with a prophet's judgment. "You have heard that it was said of old time, but I say to you," was typical of his outlook. It was not always clear whether the kingdom was within or without, in the present or the future, but it certainly was not in the past. Rather it seemed to be, at least in its beginnings, subjective and present, but it extended from thence on into a universal kingdom beyond the limits of time and space. His look was forward—not backward.[13]

Confucius recognized in himself weakness—imperfections. To this or that he often declared, "I have not attained. " Jesus—at least the Jesus of John—can say, "He that hath seen me hath seen the Father."

The East has found in Confucius a wise guide.

---

[13] A friendly critic says that the contrast between the two must not be overstressed. Confucius did look to the past, he asserts, but with the view to interpreting the present and preparing for a better future. Perhaps he is right.

The West has found in Jesus not only a guide—a way-shower—but also a Savior.

One wonders how Jesus and Confucius would regard each other if they were to meet. I suspect that it would be much the same as the meeting of Confucius and Lao-tzu. Neither would quite understand the other, although Jesus would have had a greater understanding of Confucius than Lao-tzu had. For, while Jesus now and then found it necessary, or at least helpful, to withdraw from the world in order to nourish His spiritual life through communion with the Source of all life, He always returned to the world, and in His contacts with the world He would find much of the practical advice of the Sage supremely useful in the pursuit of His chief end, the establishment of the Kingdom of God on earth as it is in Heaven.

7

Jesus and Lao-tzu

—————□—————

THERE IS NOT MUCH THAT CAN BE SURELY AFFIRMED ABOUT Lao-tzu. Historically, he is known as the founder of Taoism. Older scholars, relying chiefly upon the famous Chinese historian Ssu-ma Ch'ien, thought of him as an older contemporary of Confucius, born in 602 B. C., while the latter's birth is usually given as 551 B. C. Indeed, Ssu-ma Ch'ien says that once they met, but that they did not speak the same language and quite failed to understand each other. After an interview with the "Old Philosopher," Confucius went away puzzled, saying: "I know that birds can fly. I know that fish can swim. I know that animals can run. For the running one could make nooses; for the swimming one could make nets; for the flying one could make arrows. As to the dragon, I know not how he can bestride wind and clouds when he heavenward rises. Today I saw Lao-tzu. Is he perhaps like the dragon?"

H. G. Creel, in his *Chinese Thought from Confucius to Mao Tse-tung*, refuses even to speak about Lao-tzu as an historical figure, but discusses the thought of Taoism as that of the *Tao teh Ching* and the *Chwang-tzu*. And, it may be said also, he regards neither of these basic sources of Taoism as the work of a single author. He prefers simply to drop the problem of the man, as an historical figure, and to consider only the book.[1]

Later scholars are very certain that the Chinese historian's account is quite unhistorical. Arthur Waley asserts that his brief story of the Taoist sage is a mixture of fact and legend about, not one, but several ancient worthies, including a sage, Lao Lai-tzu, Grandfather P'eng—the Chinese Methuselah—and an historical figure, Lao-Tan, who served as treasurer of the Chou state in about 374 B. C.[2] He sums up his opinion by declaring that the Ssu-ma Ch'ien biography is really a confession that no materials at all existed for the writing of a biography.

On the other hand, Lin Yutang, who wrote the *Wisdom of Laotse* as late as 1948, asserts definitely that Lao-tzu was an historical figure who was born in 571 in K'uhsien, being an older contemporary of Confucius by twenty years, that he was the keeper of the Imperial Archives at the capital, and that he lived to about ninety years of age, leaving descendants, one of whom was later a government official. He scorns the scholars who doubt the historicity of Lao-tzu. Those who follow the scholars in regarding Taoist works as forgeries without adducing convincing evidence or exact reasoning are simply "aping a fashion now become very tiresome," he thinks.[3]

For our purposes, it does not greatly matter. Since there is so little that can be said about the person of Lao-tzu, we shall be obliged to keep the discussion largely in terms of ideas, and we shall, without attempting any serious critical analysis of the *Tao teh Ching*, simply compare its teach-

---

1 Chicago: University of Chicago Press, 1953, p. 98.

2 Allen Waley, *The Way and Its Power* (New York: Houghton Mifflin Company, 1935), pp. 106–108.

3 New York: Modern Library, Inc., 1948. Page 9.

ings with those of Jesus recorded in the Gospels. After all, it is the Jesus and Lao-tzu thus known that have had the enormous influence felt by the subsequent centuries, as I have elsewhere pointed out—not the real Jesus and Lao-tzu, if they were different from what is represented in the extant literature about them. Taoism developed in directions which its founder could hardly have foreseen, as did Christianity. We shall refer to some of these things in the course of the study.

There are, as a matter of fact, two Taoisms in China: philosophic and popular. The former may be said hardly to be a religion at all. Nor does it have an institutionalized form. It is rather a school of thought, a way of looking at the world, which finds its continuing inspiration in the study of the *Tao teh Ching* and the writings of Chwang-tzu. It has had an enormous influence on China, although less than that of Confucius. And some influence of the philosophy is, of course, evident in the organized popular Taoism as one of the three religions of China. Most of our comparison of Lao-tzu and Jesus must be drawn from the Taoist classic. There is little or nothing in popular Taoism which could be compared to advantage with the teachings of Jesus, although some marginal Christian groups would not be so far from popular Taoism today.

Jesus and Lao-tzu—the legendary Lao-tzu, if there was no real one—are alike in that wonder stories gather about them. Lao-tzu is said by one Chinese source to have been of miraculous conception, and, after 62 or 72 or 81 months in his mother's womb, to have been born with white hair. As a child, he was called sometimes the "old boy," and in later life was known as the "old philosopher." Legend makes him live, according to one story, to one hundred and twenty years; according to another, to a thousand. Jesus had a very short public life as teacher and preacher; Lao-tzu was employed for many years as keeper of the archives at the royal court. Jesus worked as an artisan, a carpenter. Lao-tzu was a white-collar government official. Jesus wrote nothing at all, leaving only living disciples who afterward contributed their memory of what He said and did to those who wrote the Gospels. As Lao-tzu was going out of the country to some unannounced destination from which he never returned, a gatekeeper who knew him besought him that he would write down his thought before leaving. He did so, and it is this which legend says we have in the Taoist classic the *Tao teh Ching*.

In many ways that are deeply significant, Jesus and Lao-tzu are alike, as we shall see, but at the same time there are deep differences. It seems not a little strange that, starting with such basically different fundamental beliefs about the ultimate questions concerning God and the universe, they should have come out so close together in practical ways. For they do differ widely in their conception of the divine. With Jesus' conception of God we are already familiar. In simple, uncomplicated fashion He assumes God's existence; that He is the creator and sustainer of the universe, and that He stands in relation to man as Father. Jesus never concerned Himself with metaphysical speculation. If He had a particular metaphysical point of view, He never dwelt upon it. God was very real, very personal, and had a Father's interest in His children and their world. This does not mean that Christians have no metaphysics: they do; indeed, there is quite a metaphysical variety among Christians, but these represent the results of later reflection rather than the views of Jesus Himself. It is from

John and Paul chiefly that later Christian thinkers draw such philosophic conclusions as they reach, insofar as these are grounded at all in the New Testament. Jesus was —whatever else He may have been— a man obsessed with a sense of mission to proclaim the good news of the coming of the Kingdom of God, and to call men to membership in it. If the Gospel of John may be taken as factual, He declared that in Himself men could see the Father. Beyond that, what else was needful?

Lao-tzu, on the other hand, was a man of definitely philosophical bent. Was he not dubbed "the old philosopher"? And his attempts at explaining the ultimate reality only succeeded in investing it with mystery—and charm. The term he uses is *Tao*. Over and over, in the little classic attributed to him, he essays to explain it, but one never gets clearly just what he means. Indeed, he says in the very opening lines of the first chapter, that the Tao which can be named is not the absolute Tao.

This resembles very closely the Hindu concept of Brahman, which can, according to a passage in the Upanishads, never be positively described. One can only say in the end of whatever is alleged of Brahman, *"neti, neti—*No, no, not that." Or it is like the term *Zen*, the name of a Buddhist sect. If, says one of the great *Zen* authorities, if you can define *Zen*, then you haven't got *Zen*, because in its very nature it completely eludes definition.

Lao-tzu says of the Tao:

> There is a thing inherent and natural
> Which existed before Heaven and earth.
> Motionless and fathomless,
> It stands alone and never changes.
> It pervades everywhere and never becomes exhausted;

It may be designated as the mother of the universe.
I do not know its name.
If I am forced to give it a name,
I call it Tao, and I name it supreme. . . .

Man follows the laws of earth;
Earth follows the laws of Heaven;
Heaven follows the laws of Tao;
Tao follows the laws of its intrinsic nature.[4]

Again he writes:

The great Tao pervades everywhere, both on the
right and the left.
By it all things come into being, and it does not reject
them. . . .
It is always nonexistent; therefore it cannot be named
as small.[5]

Or once more: "Tao is ever inactive, and yet there is
nothing that it does not do." [6] What does one make of
statements like these? Tao is elusive, intangible. It is like
trying to grasp a handful of mist. It seems never to be
personal—which, of course, differentiates it sharply from
what Jesus thought about God, for to Him God is everywhere and is always personal. The closest approach to
anything like such an idea to be found in the Gospels is in
the first chapter of John, where Jesus is identified with the
Logos which was in the beginning with God, and to be
thought of possibly as the means by which the ultimate
could be revealed in personal terms—the impersonal or the

---

[4] *Tao teh Ching*, translated by Ch'u Ta-Kao (London: The Buddhist
Society, 1937), Chapter 35. Used by permission. Also found in *The Bible of
the World*, edited by R. O. Ballou (New York: The Viking Press, 1939).

[5] *Ibid.*, Chapter 34.

[6] *Ibid.*, Chapter 37.

supra-personal made personal. But this is, of course, not from Jesus Himself, and probably not from any of the original disciples, but a bit of reflective thinking by an early second-century believer who was trying to fit Jesus into the thinking of the Greeks.

Yet, despite these very vague and cryptic descriptions of the Tao, one does now and then find that the Tao does function actively in the affairs of the world. For example, he says:

"The Tao is the treasure of good men, and the sustainer of bad men." [7] To sustain something, if the translation here is the correct one, is to act. How can the nonexistent and the inactive be said to act? Indeed, he continues in another place:

"Let the Tao reign over the world, and no spirits will show their ghostly powers." [8] In another passage he says: "The Tao of Heaven does not contend; yet it surely wins the victory." [9]

Of course, in popular Taoism, God does become quite personal and concrete. Indeed, it is a luxuriant polytheism in which Lao-tzu himself becomes a leading figure.

It is true that Lao-tzu does suggest that man finds his salvation through relating himself to the Tao. There are references to "honoring the Tao," [10] "following the Tao," [11] "walking in the great way or Tao," [12] "deviating from the Tao," [13] "applying the Tao to himself and family," [14] "pursuing the Tao," [15] "losing the Tao," [16] "identifying oneself with the Tao," [17] and "attaining the

---

[7] *Ibid.*, Chapter 62.
[8] *Ibid.*, Chapter 60.
[9] *Ibid.*, Chapter 73.
[10] *Ibid.*, Chapter 51.
[11] *Ibid.*, Chapter 52.
[12] *Ibid.*, Chapter 53.

[13] *Ibid.*, Chapter 53.
[14] *Ibid.*, Chapter 54.
[15] *Ibid.*, Chapter 48.
[16] *Ibid.*, Chapter 38.
[17] *Ibid.*, Chapter 23.

Tao." It is this last which seems to be the ultimate salvation of man. "He who attains Tao is everlasting, though
the body may decay, he never perishes." [18]

Again, they differ fundamentally in their attitudes
toward the world. Taoism, as reflected in the *Tao teh
Ching*, is essentially "world-fleeing"; Christianity, world-
embracing. To be sure, there has been an element of world
flight in Christianity in some of its branches, but always it
has been a minority manifestation, as in monasticism. Nor
does it arise out of anything Jesus Himself taught or did.
Jesus led an active life in intimate contact with people—at
least during His public ministry. He did, it is true, seek
quiet and solitude on occasion, but always, apparently,
only to appear again refreshed in spirit to carry on His
work of healing and teaching. There is, so far as I can see,
no suggestion of permanent isolation from the life of the
world in anything recorded of Him in the Gospels. He was
in the world to seek actively the lost, to heal the sick, to
teach the people. One gets even a sense of urgency in the
Markan narrative, with its frequent statements such as "and
straightway," "on the morrow," and so forth. He seemed
always on the move.

To be sure, there are apocalyptic passages which look
toward a new world, a new Jerusalem. "My kingdom is
not of this world," He says. But this is only to say that
one does not find ultimate salvation in history, but both in
and beyond history. And there is no suggestion that men
should cease to live in the midst of the world life of their
day in order to benefit in the life beyond this life.

Lao-tzu, on the other hand, in the end forsook the active life and went away—we know not where. His doc-

---

[18] *Ibid.*, Chapter 16.

trine of *wu wei,* or non-action, does not find any parallel in Jesus' teaching, save at one or two points later to be noted. In Lao-tzu, it may be said to be a central doctrine. It is insisted upon throughout the Taoist scripture. In one place he says: "By non-action everything can be done." [19] Again, "Tao is ever inactive, yet there is nothing it does not do." [20] The power of non-action is clearly seen by the use of illustration of muddy water.[21] How can it be cleared save by doing nothing about it? No amount of stirring or agitation will avail to clear it. But let it alone, and it will become perfectly clear of itself. Of course, Lao-tzu knew nothing about modern means of filtration.

It is difficult to fit such a doctrine into the ongoing life of a people. It would seem to call for the abandonment of the life in society for a life of solitude apart from other people. In government, for example, it would lead to anarchy: certainly even if observed only in a general way, it would mean that the least government is the best government. This may be seen in various passages from the *Tao teh Ching.*

> One must rule the empire by meddling with no
>   business,
> The empire can be ruled by meddling with no
>   business.   . . .
>
> The more restrictions and avoidance in empire,
> The poorer become the people;
> The more laws and regulations,
> The more robbers and thieves there are.
> Therefore the sage says:
> Inasmuch as I betake myself to non-action,
> The people of themselves become developed.[22]

---

[19] *Ibid.,* Chapter 48.
[20] *Ibid.,* Chapter 37.
[21] *Ibid.,* Chapter 15.
[22] *Ibid.,* Chapter 57, *passim.*

Or again:

> When the government is blunt and inactive, the
> people will be happy and prosperous.[23]

Jesus had very little to say about government beyond
the rather cryptic remark made to those who sought to
trap him in a dilemma which would earn him either the
hostility of the Jews on the one hand or the Roman government on the other. When they asked him if it were lawful
to pay taxes to Ceasar, he demanded of them a coin.
"Whose is the image and superscription?" he asked them.
"Caesar's," was the answer. "Then render unto Caesar the
thing that are Caesar's and to God the things that are
God's." [24]

Yet differing with respect to action and non-action, Jesus
and Lao-tzu do nevertheless come out agreeing in some
important practical ways, as we shall see. One very notable
point of agreement is in their doctrine of returning good
for evil. Thus, Jesus in the Sermon on the Mount says:
"I say unto you, love your enemies"; "if any strike you on
one cheek, turn to him the other"; "bless those who curse
you." [25]

Lao-tzu says simply: "Return love for great hatred." [26]
Or again:

> To the good I act with goodness,
> To the bad I also act with goodness.
> Thus goodness is attained.
> To the faithful I act with faith,
> To the faithless I also act with faith.
> Thus faith is attained.[27]

---

[23] *Ibid.*, Chapter 58.
[24] Matthew 22:21.
[25] Matthew 5:44.

[26] The *Tao teh Ching*, *op. cit.*, Chapter 69.
[27] *Ibid.*, Chapter 49.

Jesus and Lao-tzu are closer together than are Lao-tzu and Confucius, who said, you will recall: "The evil I requite with justice, the good I requite with good." [28]

Lao-tzu's doctrine naturally led him to a pacifist position. Non-action could never properly issue in war, for war is the most intense kind of activity in which men engage. This might lead one to classify Lao-tzu's pacifism rather as passivism, for the modern pacifists like to draw a sharp distinction between the two. They are alike, to be sure, in their non-participation in war, but passivism is a negative approach to the problem, while true pacifism is positive. It is rather to make peace, but by non-violent methods.

Did Lao-tzu never countenance war? There is one passage which can be interpreted as making a place for participating in defensive war, just as in the words of Jesus can be found an occasional word which is interpreted by some as making a place for war, such as, "I come not to bring peace but a sword." [29] But the two, whether on the same grounds or not, are upholders of a revolutionary attitude in respect to the employment of violent retaliation against evil on the part of the one who suffers it. Whether they are wrong or right in this may be a matter of difference of opinion. That they both held it, and in the case of Jesus that he certainly practiced it, seems beyond question. Lao-tzu says: [30]

> So far as arms are concerned, they are implements of ill omen. They are not implements for the man of Tao. For the actions of arms will be well re-

[28] Arthur Waley, *The Analects of Confucius* (London: George Allen and Unwin, 1938), Bk. 14:36.
[29] Matthew 10:34.
[30] *Tao teh Ching, op. cit.,* Chapter 31.

quited: where armies are quartered brambles and
thorns grow. Great wars are followed by years of
scarcity.

Both Jesus and Lao-tzu emphasized humility. "Blessed
are the meek," said Jesus, "for they shall inherit the
earth." [31] "He who would be great among you shall be
your servant." [32] "Whoever exalteth himself shall be humbled, and he who humbleth himself shall be exalted." [33]

Lao-tzu echoes the same sentiment:

Be humble and you will remain entire. . . .
The sage does not display himself, therefore he
shines.
He does not approve himself, therefore he is noted.
He does not praise himself, therefore he has merit.
He does not glory in himself, therefore he excels.[34]

Or again:

The noble must be styled in the terms of the humble,
The high must take the low as their foundation. . . .
The highest fame is to have no fame,
The kings are increased by being diminished.[35]

Both Jesus and Lao-tzu are fond of paradoxical sayings.
In this statement, which is repeated in various ways by
Lao-tzu, may be recognized a close similarity, in spirit if
not in actual language, to some of Jesus' sayings:

The weakest things in the world can overmatch the
strongest things in the world.
Nothing can be compared to water for its weak and
yielding nature,

---

[31] Matthew 5:5.
[32] Matthew 20:26.
[33] Matthew 23:12.
[34] Tao teh Ching, op. cit., Chapter 22, passim.
[35] Ibid., Chapter 39.

Yet in attacking the hard and strong, nothing proves
better than it. . . .
The weak can overcome the strong, and the yielding
can overcome the hard.[36]

In the manner of their deaths, of course, Jesus and Lao-
tzu differ. With that of Jesus on the cross we are all
familiar; no one knows of Lao-tzu's final end: he went
away and left the world, and that is the end of the story.

Philosophic Taoism has developed little or nothing of a
belief about Lao-tzu or his work. The philosophy has been
carried on, commented upon, and taught by influential followers—most outstanding of all, the mystic Chwang-tzu
—without any special reference to the founder, other than
reverence and respect for him.

Religious Taoism, on the other hand, which developed
after the beginning of the Christian era, has raised him to
the status of divinity, and made him a member of the Taoist
Trinity. And there is a definite worship of the gentle sage
as God. By some he is regarded as the incarnation of the
highest god of the Taoist pantheon, Yu Huang, the Jade
Emperor.

China is not exclusivist in its religious loyalties. Polytheistic in general, it has little difficulty in assimilating men
as gods, or gods from other lands. So it has done honor to
three great figures who have deeply affected Chinese life
by associating Confucius, Lao-tzu, and Buddha together
in a kind of a Trinity. Thus, three men, one of whom
made his own faith quite independent of gods, another
who was largely, although not altogether, humanistic in
his thought, and another whose idea of God was as intangible and elusive as the Hindu Brahman, are today often

---

[36] *Ibid.*, Chapter 78.

represented together as themselves forming a trinity of Chinese gods.

The Taoist faith has become highly decadent in recent times, and plays no great role in Chinese life; but the philosophy of Taoism lives on among some Chinese, and may yet exercise a profound influence on Chinese life.

8

Jesus and Zoroaster

———————□———————

A GREAT DEAL IS KNOWN ABOUT ZOROASTRIANISM, OR THE religion of Zoroaster. Although it is no longer a religion of great importance—it has fewer members than a number of rather small American sects, about 120,000—it has had a great past and has exercised a very large influence upon the Hebrew-Christian faith. Confined chiefly now to a small area around Bombay, India, with a remnant of a few thousands, known as Gabars, in Persia, the land of its birth, it stands halfway between the great religions of the past and the great faiths by which mankind today lives. There is a great Zoroastrian sacred literature, and there is an extensive literature about the faith; but there is little in the way of authentic information about the founder, with whom we are here concerned.

Imbedded in a literature of much later date are a number of *Gathas,* as they are called, which scholars rather generally regard as authentic writings that come from the prophet himself. In them is to be found little or no factual information concerning him; but if they are authentic expressions of the prophet, they are a priceless source for his major ideas and attitudes, and that is the really important consideration.

In comparison with the information concerning Jesus afforded in the Gospels, there is very little that is preserved that does not come from sources so far removed in time from his historic appearance in Iran that it must be considered as largely legendary rather than factual. Indeed, there is so little that a few scholars, although their numbers diminish yearly, have stoutly denied that there ever was an historic Zoroaster. Of course, this has been alleged also of Jesus.

No other founder of religions is so difficult to date. A distinguished Parsi, or Zoroastrian, speaks casually of his having appeared eight thousand five hundred years ago, that is, something over six thousand B. C. Others—among them James Hope Moulton—say that he belongs to about the time of David in Israel or Homer in Greece—some 1000 years B. C. The first Greek writer to mention Zoroaster places him about 1800 B. C., or six hundred years before the Trojan war. Berosus, the Babylonian historian, asserts that it was Zoroaster who established a Babylonian dynasty about 2000 B. C. One European scholar simply says that he lived not later than 475 B. C., while several authorities, taking their cue from a statement in a late Pahlavi scripture to the effect that he appeared 258 years before Alexander the Great, fix 660-583 B. C. as the probable date. Still other scholars think that 630-553 B. C. fits better with all the facts.

But if reliable historical and biographical data are lacking, there is no lack of legendary lore. Some of this is to be found in the *Avesta* itself. The Pahlavi Dinkhart is especially valuable, but much of the source material is non-canonical. The *Zaratusht Namah*, coming from the thirteenth century A. D., is probably the most prolific in its details with respect to his birth, childhood, and the early years of his ministry.[1]

On the basis of scripture and tradition, how, then, do Jesus and Zoroaster compare?

To begin with, the coming of both is said to have been foretold: in the case of Zoroaster, as much as three thousand years before. The *Zaratusht Namah* tells of a terrible dream his mother had before his birth of being literally torn open by wolves and the child taken from her womb, while the wolves were unable to injure him. The child comforted his mother, assuring her that God was his protector. A great hill descended from heaven and angel forms sprang forth, drove away the savage beasts, and restored the child to her womb. An astrologer sought out the mother and told her that her son would be "great, virtuous, and wise."

Various miracles attended the birth of Zoroaster. A divine light shone round about the house where he was born. As he issued from the womb, he burst into laughter. All other children cry first at birth, but he laughed. Noting this, his father cried, "This is the glory of God." All evil spirits are said to have fled into the underworld when he was born. Evil magicians sought vainly to destroy him. A shah or king, like Herod, sought to slay him. He saw the child "with a face like the early spring, beaming with the glory of God." But the hand which held the dagger with which he sought to stab him simply withered—and he failed in his attempt on the child's life.

Later Zoroaster was thrown by enemies into a raging fire—but, to the great joy of his mother, was quite unin-

[1] A translation of this is to be found in John Wilson, *The Parsis* (Bombay, 1843), Vol. II, Appendix A, pp. 477-533.

jured. Rather, he simply fell quietly asleep. Again, he was placed in a road where a herd of oxen would trample him to death, but the largest ox of them all came and stood over him, thus protecting him. Likewise a horse in a herd of horses which might have destroyed his life. When he was thrown to a pack of female wolves whose cubs had been killed, they refused to attack him. Cattle—ordinarily fearful of wolves—came among them and gave milk to the child, thus preserving him.

Of his youth—the hidden years—of which there is no information in canonical sources, there are stories, too, somewhat similar to some of the New Testament apocryphal stories of Jesus. Miracles abound in this non-canonical literature.

When at thirty years of age—at about the same age as Jesus—he began his public ministry, he desired to go to Iran. Reaching the sea, he found no ship; but, says the story, his party entered the water without removing their clothes, and "as a vessel moves with the stream, so moved they in the water of the sea. You would say a bridge had been formed and that I crossed quickly thereon." Later, another bit of water—a "deep sea without a bottom"— was miraculously crossed.

Thus far, these are all legendary stories of his birth and childhood and youth. What we actually know is very little. His father's name was Pouruhaspa ("with gray horses") his mother Dughdova ("who has milked cows"). He married and had children. His daughter is mentioned in a nuptial ode in the *Gathas*. Her name was Pourucista ("very thoughtful"). This seems to be quite in line with Zoroaster's emphasis on Good Thought (Vohu Manah). He seems to have left home at about 15 years of age and wandered far in the next 15 years seeking an answer to the deeper questions which arose in his mind. Some of these are echoed in one of the *Gathas*, in which Zoroaster, having been admitted to the presence of Ahura Mazda, asks, "How should I pray?" "Who was the father of Justice?" "Who sustains the earth and the clouds, that they do not fall?" "Who is the creator of Good Disposition?" "Does love support justice?" "Is the message I am to proclaim genuine?" "What are thy purposes?" "How shall I carry them out?"

It was this experience of being led into the presence of Ahura Mazda by Good Thought, and his instruction gained there, that serve as a call to the prophet somewhat comparable to the baptismal experience of Jesus. It was after this that his public ministry really began.

But as in the case of Jesus, he underwent an experience of temptation. According to legend, Angra Mainyu, the Evil Spirit, standing over against Ahura Mazda offered Zoroaster a rich reward if he would abandon his faith in Ahura Mazda. Repeatedly the effort was made to move him, but Zoroaster steadfastly refused to yield. "Never," he cried, "shall I abjure the faith of those who worship Mazda, not if my body nor my life, nor my senses fly apart." At last the demons, discouraged by his constancy, shouted and fled away into the place of darkness from which they had come. (*Vendidad* 19: 1).

And, of course, Zoraster, like all the prophets, and like Jesus, had a deep sense of mission that drove him to seek to win the world to the worship of Ahura Mazda. He differed in his method and in the direction of his effort, as we shall presently see, but during his whole life—and he lived to more than threescore and ten—he was under a profound sense of compulsion to proclaim his Lord to men and nations.

Both Jesus and Zoroaster were believers in one God, who was at the same time ethical in character and ruled the world under a moral order which rewarded the good and punished the evil ones. Jesus appeared on the scene long after the Hebrew faith had developed a thorough-going ethical monotheism, and God was regarded as the Universal Creator and guarantor of the moral order of the world. Not so Zoroaster, who stands as a figure comparable to the prophets of perhaps the seventh or sixth century B. C.—to which, indeed, he himself probably belonged. He appeared at a time when there were many gods competing for men's loyalty, and it was his great contribution to lift one of the many to a place of supremacy and to demand that mankind worship him. That his monotheism may not have been as clear and sharp as that of Jesus is understandable. That it is profoundly ethical, there can be no doubt. His independent reaching of this insight places him high among the great religious revelators of the world, and to the Christian identifies him definitely as one of the witnesses whom God has raised up among the nations outside of the Hebrew-Christian tradition.

Both Jesus and Zoroaster believed and taught that the individual lives on after death, and that his future state is conditioned by what he has done during his earthly career. Here is no loss of individual identity in the larger soul of the world, as in Hinduism but personal, individual survival. God rewards man for his good behavior, punishes him for the evil he commits. Both faiths—Christianity as well as Zoroastrianism—developed a wealth of ideas, often divergent and even contradictory with reference to the details of the after-life, which probably go far beyond what either Jesus or Zoroaster believed or taught; but their basic beliefs in a morally conditioned ongoing individual existence are strikingly alike.

There has been a peculiarly lush development of ideas as to the details of the future life in late Zoroastrianism, which quite probably did contribute its influence to the developing ideas of Christianity in this area. We are not certain just how much of it Zoroaster himself taught. His idea is, however, very clear, even in the *Gathas*, that man, endowed with free will, makes his deliberate choice between the two warring principles of good and evil, and so determines his future destiny. Later development has the soul of the good man met after death by a beautiful maiden; the evil, by an ancient hag. Each man, by his own actions on earth, determines who shall meet him on the other side. In the *Gathas*, there is a weighing of the good and evil deeds that a man was wrought. A record of his good deeds and evil ones have been kept. If there is an excess of good, one enters the House of Song or the Abode of Good; if deficient, he goes to the House of the Lie. If they just balance, the soul goes to a separate place.

Then, although the stories do not say just when it takes place, there is, according to Zoroaster, the bridge of judgment, *Chinvat*, which souls must cross. To the evil, it narrows till it becomes as a razor's edge, and the souls fall from it into the abyss. To the righteous, it widens to become a broad highway on which they may safely cross the chasm. Finally there comes a general judgment, and all must pass through a flood of molten metal—which to the good will seem as warm milk, but to the evil a searing flame—and all evil will be purged and the world then restored to perfection.

All this is not clear or detailed in the *Gathas*, but the basis for it is there and it has been elaborated in very great detail in late Zoroastrianism. Into it there has crept a highly apocalyptic strain, like that found in Christianity. There is a real question as to the degree to which Jesus and Zoroaster themselves were apocalyptic in their outlook. By late followers, both have certainly been regarded as holding and teaching an apocalyptic view of history.

Although it is not so clear in the teaching of Zoroaster, or as central as in that of Jesus, Zoroaster does speak of the Kingdom of God. A. V. W. Jackson speaks of it thus:

> In the Gathas themselves, the pious expectation of a new order of things is the motif upon which Zoroaster rings continual changes. A mighty crisis is impending; every man ought to choose the right and seek to attain the ideal state; mankind shall then become perfect, and the world renovated. This event will be the establishment of the power and dominion of Good over evil; it will be the beginning of the complete rule of the sovereignty divine—"the Kingdom" or "the Good Kingdom" as it is called. It is in the coming of this blessed era that the resurrection of the dead will take place. A general judgment is to follow and this will be accompanied by a flood of molten metal in which the wicked shall be punished, the righteous cleansed, and evil be banished forever from the earth.[2]

At what points do they differ? As already stated, Zoroaster was married—indeed, three times—and had several children. According to tradition, he lived to the age of 77—nearly a half-century longer than Jesus. A very late tradition asserts that he met a violent death while praying

---

[2] A. V. W. Jackson, *Zoroastrian Studies* (New York: Columbia University Press, 1928), pp. 143–144.

in a fire temple. So, in respect to the outward circumstances, their lives were very different.

They differed in the way they went about proclaiming their message. Jesus worked mainly with the ordinary people of his day and had no contact with the rulers of his time, save as he was judged by them. Zoroaster seems to have worked from the top down. Certainly he achieved little success in his ministry until he had managed to convert Vishtaspa, whom legend represents as a powerful king, to his new faith. After that the going was easier. Zoroaster did have a concern for the poor. He seems to have preached a kind of brotherhood, but in his ministry generally he had the support of government. Jesus clashed with the government of his day and was crucified by it.

Zoroaster stands in rather sharp contrast to Jesus in his apparent acceptance and even employment of force as a necessity. Jesus' attitude, on the basis of all save two or three sayings, which have sometimes been interpreted as sanctioning the use of violence—for example, the cleansing of the temple, and his declaration "I am come not to bring peace but a sword"—was consistently that of passive resistance or non-violence. The record of his own behavior, aside from the very mild use of a whip chord in driving the animals from the temple, presents him as completely non-violent. Certainly there was no killing either of animals or of men involved in this episode.

Yet I was struck by a statement of an Indian Parsi, who evidently was himself a follower of Ghandi in his non-violent resistance to Great Britain's rule in India, that non-violence is clearly taught in the *Gathas*. He cites a saying which he translates thus: "Asa gave the reply '*with righteousness which is always non-violent and without malice.*'" He comments: "There can be no righteousness if there is any kind of violence in thought, word or deed." [3] It may be, I suggest, that this represents, rather, the ideas of this modern Parsi leader, read back into the record. There is not much that can be brought to its support out of the little we know about the prophet. It scarcely seems likely that, with such an outlook, he could have secured the support of the powerful Vishtaspa, who, as legend represents him, certainly was in no sense nonviolent in his own conduct or in that of his kingdom. Believers are exhorted in the *Gathas* to chastise with the sword the unbelievers, and the preoccupation with religious wars in the later literature attests to the fact of a militant rather than passivist early faith.

Zoroaster seems to differ sharply with Jesus' attitude of overcoming evil with good. He declared, "He who is good to an evil person becomes evil himself." [4] Again, he said, "Whoso worketh ill for the liar by word or thought or hands, or converts his dependents to the good, such men meet the will of Ahura Mazda to his satisfaction." [5]

While we observed substantial agreement between Jesus and Zoroaster in respect to the idea of God, it must be noted that there were differences between them. We have already suggested that the monotheism of Jesus was more sharply drawn than that of Zoroaster. Perhaps, in the strict construction of monotheism as belief in one and only one God or divine being, Zoroaster would not qualify at all, although it is true that no other God than Ahura Mazda is mentioned in the *Gathas*. It all depends on how the six

---

[3] Ardeshir Franyi Khabardar, in *New Light on the Gathas* (Bombay, 1951), pp. 54 ff.

[4] *Yasna* 46:6. It should be said that in another translation this reads: "He is evil who in the sight of the evil one is best." It is an admittedly difficult passage.

[5] *Ibid.*, 33:2.

Amesha Spentas are to be understood. They are always associated with Ahura Mazda and seem almost to be separate spirits or divine beings. L. S. Mills thinks that in them we have a union reminiscent of the Sabellian Trinity. While they are unified, they are nevertheless separate. By name and often so invoked, they are *Vohu Manah*, or Good Thought; *Asha*, the divine order; *Khshathra*, or sovereign power, "realized in a kingdom of righteousness"; *Aramaiti*, Piety or Devotion; *Haurvatat*, or "God's perfection," said to be consummated through his "truth, love, power and vital energy"; and finally Immortality, *Ameretat*.[6] Sometimes these are regarded as Archangels, and are usually personified. Just how Zoroaster himself thought of them, it is not easy to say— but it is definitely a fact that in later times they were considered as divine beings, subordinate to but having separate existence apart from Ahura Mazda.

The strong belief in the adversary, Angra Mainya or Ahriman, by Zoroaster may not be different save in the degree of emphasis from what is found in Jesus' references to Satan. Both are spoken of as though personal in character, although by neither was there any cult of the power of evil. Both Judaism and Christianity, along with Zoroastrianism, are practical dualisms—this perhaps being forced upon them by their conviction of the ethical character of God and the necessity of attributing evil to other than the good God. Certainly Zoroaster was obsessed more deeply with the idea of the conflict between God or Good and the evil forces of the world than was Jesus—although their later followers sound very much alike, especially in

---

[6] L. S. Mills, *Our Own Religion in Ancient Persia* (Chicago: Open Court Publishing Company, 1913), pp. 12 ff.

respect to the last days, when evil will be destroyed and only the good remain.

Salvation, according to Zoroaster, was something man earned by his own good works. To be sure, Zoroaster felt called by God to preach righteousness to men and to encourage them to do the works necessary for salvation. In this sense, God takes the initiative, and this may be regarded as in itself an act of Grace. But he did not, as Jesus did, call men to repentance; nor did he preach the forgiveness of sins. An eminent Zoroastrian, J. C. D. Pavry, specifically declares that Zoroaster himself had no place for a real remission of sins, although later Zoroastrianism does.[7] There was certainly no doctrine of the atonement in Zoroaster's teaching, no giving his life as a ransom for many. Good deeds offset bad deeds; good thoughts, bad thoughts; good words, bad words. Man determined his ultimate destiny by his own choice. If at the jugment his evil deeds outweighed his good, then he went the Place of the Lie; if the good overbalanced the evil, he went to the House of Song. If they were in exact balance, a special place was reserved for him until the resurrection and final judgment, when the evil would be purged by fire. It is not always possible to say that these detailed ideas go back to Zoroaster himself, but they are found in those who came after him.

How did his later followers think of Zoroaster? That he thought of himself as a reformer and prophet seems quite clear. As we have seen, it is not so clear just how Jesus regarded himself. On the basis of the synoptics, it is possible to come to one conclusion; on the basis of

_____

[7] J. C. D. Pavry, *Zoroastrian Doctrine of the Future Life* (New York: Columbia University Press, 1926), p. 13.

John's gospel, to quite another. The varying Christologies that have been held are a witness to the difficulty of making an exact assertion concerning the question.

Generally speaking, Zoroaster's role has been considered that of a prophet—not a divinity. Thus, a modern educated Parsi writer says:

> He was the man amongst men. . . . He had everything that is great and good in men. He was the fountain of pity and truth. He was the friend, not only of the poor and the weak, but also of dumb-driven cattle. He was the living lighted fountain, the light which enlightens the darkness of the world, and this not a kindled lamp only, but rather as a natural luminary shining by the gift of nature; a glowing light-fountain of Nature, of native original insight, of manhood and heroic nobleness in whose radiance all souls feel that it is well with them.[8]

The wealth of legendary lore that grew up about Zoroaster, replete with miracles attendant upon his birth and later development, is a witness to the fact that he was regarded in very much the same way that later followers regarded Jesus, who was clearly deified by them. Late Zoroastrianism undoubtedly regards its founder as the key figure in the salvation of man and the ending of the world. It represents history as of 12,000 years' duration, which are divided into four periods of 3,000 years each. The first was the era of spiritual creation, in which the whole creation was brought into being, but only in a spiritual state. In the second period, the material creation was effected: the sky, water, earth, plants, animal life, and man came into existence. In the third, Ahriman irrupts

---

[8] E. Divecha, *Modern Thought and Zoroaster* (Bombay: Popular Press, n. d.), p. 21.

into the created world; evil spirits assault man and his world. The last period is that from the appearance of Zoroaster to the end of the world. The seed of Zoroaster, miraculously preserved in a Lake Kasava, will impregnate two virgins who bathe in its waters, and his posthumous sons, thus virgin-born, will be saviors and at the end usher in the new and perfect era. The forces of evil being destroyed, Zoroaster prophesies the coming *Saoshyant*, or savior, but the details of his coming are the product of a later period.

I have not found prayers addressed to Zoroaster, but he is said by Pavry to be "the one who will judge men on their life record and will act as Judge, both at the individual and at the general judgment" at the end.[9] That is, he occupies something of the position assigned to Jesus in the Apostles' Creed: "from whence he shall come to judge the quick and the dead."

In a rock carving, not far from the city of Kermanshah, there are three figures standing and one prostrate. The first of the three is a figure which stands out from the rest by having what seem to be rays of light emanating from his head. This is by some scholars identified as Zoroaster. If this be a correct identification, this special symbol of light surrounding his head puts him in somewhat the same character as Jesus, in paintings of Him, where the head is surrounded by a halo, and may indicate a tendency to deify Zoroaster.

Probably at the popular level, this has often enough been done. At the level of the modern intellectual, Zoroaster is a prophet who brought to man a new religion, which Divecha summarizes thus:

---

[9] Pavry, *op. cit.*, p. 57.

It teaches that happiness and misery are the fruits of man's own sowing, and therefore wants man to look first to others, especially the weak and the poor, including the dumb-driven cattle, and to do his duty for duty's sake. It wants man to be good to the good and relentless to the wicked. It sees no difference between a tiger and a tyrant, as neither is worthy of living . . . Being a natural religion, it is based on love and believes in the equality and brotherhood of man . . . It teaches that "that alone is good for one which is good for all." [10]

And Pavry, a Zoroastrian scholar, expresses what he regards as the essential heart of Zoroastrianism—at least, early Zoroastrianism—thus:

Faith and works form the foundation of the doctrine of salvation in the religion of ancient Iran. A belief in the freedom of the will, in the acknowledgment of man's ability to choose the right or choose the wrong, and in his consequent responsibility to his Creator, lies at the basis of the moral and ethical system of the Zoroastrian religion, which above all emphasizes the existence of two warring principles of Good and Evil, Light and Darkness. To guide man to the choice of right, and thus to assure his gaining eternal salvation, was the very purpose of Zoroaster's mission upon earth.[11]

Certainly Zoroaster and Jesus at the human level were kindred spirits, outstanding figures in a long line of those who felt called upon to speak to mankind in the name of God and call them to choose His way as theirs, believing that therein lay man's salvation and that of his world.

[10] Divecha, *op. cit.*, p. 17.
[11] Pavry, *op. cit.*, pp. 26–27.

9

Jesus and Moses

JUDAISM AND CHRISTIANITY HAVE OFTEN ENOUGH BEEN compared—by both Jews and Christians. But I have never seen a published comparison of Jesus and Moses. Christians, of course, regard Moses as belonging quite as much to themselves as to the Jews. Indeed, John Haynes Holmes once wrote an article in which he intimated that the Christian world had stolen the Old Testament and many of its members were resentful that Jews should claim it as their own. If Moses, then, belongs also to Christianity, why make a comparison of him with Jesus, beyond perhaps saying that Jesus was the fulfilment of everything Moses contributed by way of law to the faith? Did not Jesus say, "I came not to destroy the law but to fulfill it"?

In making a comparison of Jesus and Moses, we shall not be comparing Judaism and Christianity, for Judaism is much more than Moses and the law. It is also the prophets and the sages; the singers and poets of Israel—just as Christianity is more than Jesus: being also Paul, the Apostles, the Church Fathers, the pope, Martin Luther, John Wesley, Billy Graham, and the World Council of Churches.

But, in a real sense, both Jesus and Moses were founders,

respectively, of Christianity and Judaism. They were the starting point of two very definite historical religious movements, and as such may well be compared. The prophets added enormously to what Moses brought his people, and Jesus stands directly in the tradition of the prophets. In a sense we shall, in contrasting Jesus and Moses, be contrasting the legal and the prophetic strains in Judaism itself, for it was over against Moses, as symbolizing the legal aspects of Judaism, that Jesus as prophet stands out as so strikingly different.

The sources for the understanding of Moses are several, that is, the Moses as he has come to be thought of within Judaism. First of all, there is the Pentateuch, or the Torah, the so-called Books of Moses—the most basic source of all. But there are also numerous references in other parts of the Bible. It was interesting to me to observe the number of times his name appears after the first five books. In Joshua, following immediately after, it occurred 56 times, but only 52 times in all the remaining Old Testament books. In the New Testament, it appeared 105 times. In almost all cases, the reference was incidental in such phrases as "Moses said," "the law of Moses," "the Book of Moses," "the Lord spake to Moses saying," "Moses commanded," and so forth. Twenty-eight times he was characterized as "servant of the Lord," four times as "Man of God," once "His chosen." Practically nothing is told about him that is not already told in the Pentateuch. Only once, in Jude, is there a reference that goes beyond the historical, where Jude speaks of the archangel Michael contending with the devil, disputing the body of Moses.

A second source is the Talmud, which is, of course, full of references to Moses, many of them revealing the growth of tradition about him. Some of the more fascinating bits about Moses come from this source.

Third, there is a considerable amount of non-Talmudic literature—rabbinical writings both of Palestinian and Hellenistic background which carry legendary material concerning the great lawgiver. A very interesting popular account of Moses, drawing from these later sources, is the book, *The Life of Moses*,[1] by Edmond Fleg. Sholem Asch, in his *Moses*,[2] likewise is indebted in some degree to these non-Biblical sources.

How much of what is known about Moses has a real historical basis? Probably none of the sources, at least in their present form, are contemporary. Conservative scholarship attributes the Pentateuch, of course, to Moses himself, but modern critical scholars are of the opinion that the books in their present form are the end result of a long literary process involving original variant oral traditions, finally written down in separate documents, and later fused together into the present books, the completion of the process having been delayed until the post-exilic period under Ezra. If this is so, how much dependence can be placed upon such information as they carry concerning Moses and the events with which he is connected?

As in the case of most great men of antiquity, including Jesus, critics have arisen to doubt his very historic existence. But, so far as I know, no reputable historian any longer doubts that back of the figure of either Jesus or Moses there was a genuine historical figure who, if he did not indeed do and say everything as reported, did by his appearance, and what he said and did, prove to be the

---

[1] Edmond **Fleg**, *The Life of Moses* (New York: E. P. Dutton & Co., 1928).
[2] Sholem **Asch**, *Moses* (New York: G. P. Putnam's Sons, 1951).

effective starting point of a great new faith. What we shall be dealing with in this brief comparison is the two figures as they have crystallized out in the traditions of their followers, for I believe it is true that it is these accounts and these ideas which really affect men today, regardless of whether they are grounded at every point in literal fact. Moses and Jesus influence men now—and this has been so since the closing of the Old Testament and New Testament canons—not by what they were and said, but what it is reported and men now believe that they did and said.

A minimum view concerning Moses by the most critical minds makes him a real, if dim, historical figure who appeared in Egypt in the thirteenth century B.C., probably; led at least a part of the Hebrew people out of Egypt; introduced certain basic laws; and effected a rather radical reform in their religion. It is difficult to account for his great reputation as lawgiver and leader otherwise. Sigmund Freud,[3] who could hardly be called a scholar in this field, advances the interesting idea that Moses was not a Hebrew at all, but an Egyptian—an ardent follower of Akhnaton, the Pharaoh who first introduced the Egyptians to monotheism. Disappointed by the failure of Akhnaton's reform among the Egyptians, he thinks, Moses introduced his idea to the Hebrews and led them out of Egypt.

In the Biblical story we are all acquainted with, Moses, after fleeing Egypt, became a shepherd in Midian; saw the burning bush; was called of God to lead the people out of Egypt, which he did; gave them the law received at the hands of God at Mt. Sinai; and introduced to them the

---

[3] Sigmund Freud, *Moses and Monotheism* (New York: Alfred A. Knopf, Inc., 1939).

unique worship of Yahweh. In the light of our present Biblical story, this appears as no innovation, since Abraham and the other patriarchs were all worshippers of one God. According to many modern critical scholars, the monotheism of Abraham *et al.* is the result of the projection of later-developed ideas back into pre-Mosaic times. But he did give the God a new name. "By this name have I not been known in Israel," God said to him. Moses led the people as far as the Jordan, but was not permitted to enter the promised land. "His burial place no man knoweth."

On the basis of these sources, how are Jesus and Moses alike and how do they differ? First the resemblances.

Well, to begin with, unusual birth stories gather about both of them. In the case of Jesus, I shall assume a knowledge of them without recounting them. In the Bible itself, Moses' birth is announced simply: "The woman conceived and bore a son." (Exodus 2:2.) She was the proper wife of a Levite, Amram, so the birth was quite a normal one, as compared with Jesus' virgin birth, according to Matthew and Luke. But there had been prophecies. According to a Rabbinical tale, Miriam, sister of Moses, prophesied to his father the birth of a son who would lead Israel out of Egypt. Also, according to legend, Pharaoh had been told of it by soothsayers, and this resulted in his order to drown all male children. Compare Herod's ordering the killing of male children in order to bring about the certain death of the Christ Child who would be King of the Jews. In the case of Moses, it is said that at his birth a glorious light filled the house. He was born already circumcised. He was able to take off and walk at birth. He talked with his father on his first day, and at three days of age he began to prophesy.

In both cases, the child who was prophesied was saved from being destroyed by a king. Joseph and Mary fled into Egypt to save the young Child's life; Moses' mother hid him in a basket in the Nile, where he was found and adopted by a princess within the royal household. Dr. William A. Irwin points out that there is a widespread legend, which he calls the legend of the abandoned baby, in which a baby of humble origin, cast out to die, is miraculously or otherwise saved, then grows up to be the leader or savior of his people. It is best known, perhaps, in the story of Sargon of Akkad, and of Romulus and Remus in Roman history.

A great deal of the miraculous element is associated with both Moses and Jesus. In the case of the latter, there is nothing of anything miraculous occurring during His childhood told in the four gospels, although there are a great many stories of childhood miracles in the apocryphal gospels. Nor is there any record of childhood miracles of Moses in the Biblical narrative. But in tradition there are not a few. Notable is the one which tells that Pharaoh's daughter was afflicted with leprosy, for which there was no cure, even for royalty. But when she touched the child, Moses, in his basket among the reeds, lo, the leprosy left her and she was healed. Also, it is narrated that the 600,000 children thrown into the river to be drowned were miraculously saved and restored to life because of Moses.

Another tale is that after killing the Egyptian, Moses was condemned to death by Pharaoh and delivered to the executioner, but his neck suddenly became as a pillar of marble, dulling the edge of the executioner's sword. The angel Michael then took the sword, assumed the form of the executioner, giving the latter Moses' form, and slew him.

Moses, according to tradition, fled to Ethiopia and became a king there, but after forty years went to Midian. In the garden of Jethro was a tree which had been the staff of Adam. Jethro offered Zipporah, his daughter, in marriage to anyone who would pull it up. Moses did so with ease, and this was the rod he carried and with which he performed miracles before Pharaoh, when demanding that the Hebrews be allowed to go free.

From the burning bush on through the rest of his life, the Bible narrates miracles wrought by Moses, just as the New Testament does concerning Jesus: the separating of the waters at the Red Sea, the plagues, manna in the wilderness, his striking the rock to provide water, and his lifting up the serpent of brass as a cure for snake bite. I need not recount those of Jesus. Both were miracle workers.

Both Moses and Jesus were great reformers. Both were innovators. Each broke sharply with his past. In the case of Jesus, this is much more evident on the basis of the Biblical sources. We cannot be so sure of what Israel was before the coming of Moses, owing, as modern scholarship thinks, to the fact that the pre-Mosaic Biblical account is, in its present form, the result of much late editing, so that ideas of a much later period have been read back into the past. The result is that Moses' ideas do not seem so strikingly new as they must actually have seemed to the Hebrews, who had not yet developed to the point credited to them by later Jewish thought. Certain it is that Moses experienced formidable opposition again and again to what he was trying to get the Hebrews to do. It is Freud's theory, based upon the interpretation of a passage in Amos by a German scholar, Sellin, that finally Moses was killed by the people in open revolt against him.

Whatever else Moses may have done, he must have been in some degree a lawgiver. It may well be doubted whether, as appears in the Pentateuch, he actually gave them all the detailed laws of the covenant code, the priest's code, the Deuteronomic code, the Holiness code, and the general Levitical laws, although conservative Jewish and Christian scholarship believes that he did. But the fact that all these laws are attributed to him seems to be prima facie evidence that he early acquired a great reputation as lawgiver. Just as Proverbs tend to be attributed to Solomon and Psalms to David, so law is attributed to Moses. And this represented innovation.

If we may believe the story of the Hebrews' long enslavement and residence among an alien people, probably much influenced by the social and religious environment in which they found themselves, the need for a set of rather rigid rules by which to live as they set forth on their nomadic wanderings of more than a generation before coming to the Promised Land, seems quite obvious. These, Moses undoubtedly gave them, and he gave them in the name of God, putting the whole authority and power of God behind them.

Probably no event in the whole life of Moses is so celebrated in story as that of his getting the Torah. Even in the Bible it is told dramatically, although, according to the Deuteronomy account, it was only the decalogue, not the Torah, that was received. Moses goes into the mountain, is hidden in the clouds. Thunder and lightning play about it, and out of the storm he descends, his face shining with a holy light, bearing the tablets of the law.

But in the legends it is magnified almost into an epic. Moses ascends into the heavens—passes through one after another, until he confronts God Himself in the sixth heaven—and receives the entire Torah directly from His hands.

As told in popular fashion in Fleg's story of Moses, it is a thrilling episode, revealing clearly the esteem in which Moses is held and the importance of the Torah which came through him from the very hand of God. When Moses went up into the mountain, a cloud enfolded him and bore him to the heavens. At the fourth heaven, he was stopped by an angel with 12,000 destroying angels. As the angel sought to seize him, Moses struck him and flung him down. On to the fifth heaven he went; there dwelt Hadarniel, whose words were as seventy thousand lightnings. The angel asked, "What comest thou to seek among the holy ones, man born of sin?" But the Voice of the Creator was heard crying, "If I do not give my Torah to man the world will return to chaos." Whereupon the archangel took Moses and led him by a path, which it would have taken a mortal five hundred years to climb, to the sixth heaven, where Sandalfon reigned. When Moses saw him, he was filled with terror; but the Holy One Himself descended from His throne, and placed His splendor between Moses and the angel so that he might pass. Then he entered the School of the Most High, where the angel Zagzagel teaches the Torah to the angels. The angels, seeing Moses, cried, "Wilt thou Zagzagel teach the Torah to this man? Will he not say to mankind, this is *my* Torah?"

Then did the Torah itself rise up—flanked by the

archangels Michael, Gabriel, Uriel, and Raphael—and cry "King of the World, hath not this man obeyed me even before knowing me? Hath he not proclaimed thy name, kept the sabbath, honored parents and turned away from lying and blasphemy, kept his soul from theft, murder, uncleanness, and envy? What matters it, Lord, if he should one day say, this is my Torah. Is it not he who obeyeth thy Torah, as if he had created it?" Then the Holy One said, "Sit thou Moses above the angels; behold I myself shall teach the Torah to thee." And the Lord taught Moses his sacred law, and because, in a moment of temptation by Satan, Moses refused to boast of possessing it, God said to him, "Since thou findest thyself small before the Torah, behold, it shall be called by thy name." Thus it is written, "Remember the Torah of Moses, my servant."

So precious was the law that it was written on tablets of sapphire.[4]

Both Jesus and Moses mark clearly new epochs in religion and history. Moses is an epoch-making figure in Israel's history—Jesus, in the history of the world itself. A great part of the world now reckons history in time as before and after Jesus' birth.

Both insisted upon the worship of but one God, who was ethically conceived, the rewarder of good and the punisher of evil. For the Hebrews, this also represented innovation. From the standpoint of modern scholarship, it certainly does, for these modern scholars think that, on the basis of an analysis of the Biblical record, they can see clearly that, before Moses, the people were probably neither worshippers of one God only, nor wholly averse to idolatry.

---

[4] Fleg, *op. cit.*, Chapter 11.

Conservative scholarship will not admit this. They will agree that Moses confirmed the people in the worship of but one God, and most will agree that Moses introduced the new name, Yahweh, as a result of his conversation with God at the burning bush, and, of course, that he strictly forbade the use of idols, indicating at least a tendency to the contrary practice as common among the surrounding peoples.

Conservative scholarship quite unanimously declares that Moses believed and taught his people a strict monotheism, that there was no other God. But this is scarcely borne out even in the Decalogue, which they fully attribute to Moses in its present form. For the commandment is only, "Thou shalt have no other gods before me." Would not this argue the possibility that other gods might exist? Many modern scholars employ the term *monolatry* to distinguish this stage of religious belief from a full monotheism. Monotheism affirms the sole existence of one God. There is no other. Later Judaism is an unquestioned monotheism. The *Shema* seems to state it: "Hear O Israel, the Lord our God is one Lord." It is only a question as to when this emerged fully. Some think it did so in Moses, some Amos, some Isaiah. Everyone admits that it is fully reached in Second Isaiah.

Liberal scholarship does not agree on the source from which Moses got the idea of one God. Was it by revelation, as declared in the Bible story of the burning bush? Or did he get it from Akhnaton, the monotheistic Pharaoh of Egypt, or was it from his father-in-law, Jethro, as held by the exponents of the so-called Kenite theory? Perhaps it will never be surely known.

At all events, it is perfectly clear that both Jesus and

Moses taught the worship of one God ethically conceived, who was the judge of men. In the case of Jesus, there can be no question that His was a fully rounded monotheistic belief, and that God was the guarantor of the moral order of the entire universe. Time, the work of the prophets, and His own insight had defined ethics in ways not found in the earlier period. But both were sure that ethics, however defined in detail, were rooted in God, the sole object of their worship. In this respect, Judaism and Christianity are in complete accord today.

Both Jesus and Moses considered themselves as sent by God in some sense to set men free, to deliver them from bondage. In the case of Moses, it was clearly to set a particular people free from human bondage, and to lead them to a new place where they could be their own masters. Moses' commission comes to him at the burning bush. Jesus begins His public life with His baptism at the hands of John. We are not told of what went on in Jesus' mind before that or what finally led Him to leave Nazareth and go down to the Jordan to be baptized. At the baptism it is said that the voice of God spoke, saying, "This is my beloved son, hear ye him." What Jesus felt is not recorded, but He went away and spent forty days apparently in intense struggle of soul represented in the temptations, then came out and began His quiet, confident ministry, preaching the good news of the Kingdom of God. Over and over He speaks of being sent—"I must work the works of Him who sent me"; "As the Father sent me"—He said to His disciples—"even so do I send you." On whatever Christological level you take it, Jesus believed that He was *sent* "that they might have life," "to seek and to save that which was lost." It is put in a great many different ways.

So far, we have seen some rather significant likenesses between Jesus and Moses. How did they differ?

Well, first of all, Jesus was born of humble parents, grew up among humble folk, and spent most of His life among them. A few times, we find Him in contact with the rich and powerful, but mostly it was with fishermen or farmers or small-town people that He spent His time. Moses was born of slave parents, but grew up in the royal court of Egypt, living in privilege and luxury, until his sympathy for the Jewish slaves led him to kill an Egyptian and he had to flee the country. He was a shepherd for a time, then leader of his people.

Jesus becomes an itinerant preacher and teacher, living familiarly among the village people, always at a very modest level. Moses leads the people. He commands. He stands apart from the people. He goes apart into the mountain to talk with Yahweh. He comes back, his face aglow; the people stand in awe of him. People press about Jesus in a crowd, seeking to touch Him. Children climb over Him. He takes them in His arms. I get the impression somehow that children would be afraid of Moses. There seems to have been something rather stern and forbidding about him.

Jesus' public career was very brief—only three years at most, probably much less. Moses led the children of Israel for forty years in the wilderness.

Both Jesus and Moses frequently communed with God. Both, in order to do so, went apart from the crowds— sought solitude. But there the similarity ceases. Jesus spent the night in prayer; He went out into the mountain or down by the sea alone, in quiet places. He seemed to do so as a source of spiritual refreshment. For Moses, the times of communion seem rather to have been—at least, as represented in both Biblical and legendary sources—for the purpose of getting the law, or for guidance as to what he was to do, and they are generally accompanied in the narratives by some natural disturbance—heavy clouds, lightning, thunder, or storm.

Moses gave the people a great body of law—that is, on the basis of the Biblical and legendary accounts. He gave not only rather general directions as in the Decalogue —a brief summary of the basic requirements laid upon Hebrews by God—but also the most detailed rules for almost every phase of their lives, economic, social, and political, as well as religious. "You shall not let your cattle breed with a different kind; you shall not sow your fields with two kinds of seed." (Lv. 19:19.) "You shall have just weights and balances." (Lv. 19:35.) "Everything in the waters that has not fins and scales is an abomination unto you." (Lv. 11:12.) "You shall not lend upon interest to your brother." (Dt. 23:19.) "You shall not muzzle an ox when it treads out the grain." (Dt. 25:4.)

Jesus, on the other hand, gave no specific laws, but, rather, broad principles. He summed up the law when asked about it by a lawyer wishing to test him. "Thou shalt love the Lord thy God with all thy heart and with all thy soul, and with all thy mind. This is the great and first commandment. And a second is like unto it, Thou shalt love thy neighbor as thyself. On these two commandments hangeth all the law and the prophets." (Matthew 22:37-40.)

The Sermon on the Mount, which is a gathering together of a great many sayings of Jesus, reported as given separately by the other Gospels, comes as close as anything in the Gospels to being a code, but it is couched in general terms: love your enemies; turn the other cheek; do not let your piety be seen of men; do not try to serve two masters; be not anxious for your life; judge not, that you be not judged; forgive men their trespasses. In the main, these are basic principles which must be wrought out in practice by the individual in situations that arise for which there is no detailed direction. How does one love his enemies? In what concrete ways can this be done?

It is true that occasional broad principles are reputed as enunciated by Moses, such as, "Thou shalt love thy neighbor as thyself" (Lv. 19:18), but the basic pattern of Mosaic law is to provide specific directions for almost every conceivable situation. And what has not been provided for in the Bible itself has been provided for in the Talmud and rabbinical tradition, although new situations still call for decision from time to time. The *Responsa* of the rabbis has developed in answer to this need.

Again, Jesus, while He gave the impulse to the creation of an organization and a cult, seems to have established no formal organization or any form of worship. I recognize that at this point there are differences of opinion. The Catholic Church believes that in the Matthew passage (Matt. 16:18), where Jesus said, "Thou art Peter, and on this rock will I build my church, and the gates of hell shall not prevail against it, . . ." He laid down the foundation of the Christian Church, which is, of course, in their view, preserved faithfully in the Roman Catholic Church. Protestants on the other hand believe that it was on Peter's confession, not Peter, that the church was to be built. Some Protestant scholars are quick to point out that only in two other places in the Gospels, both in a single verse, does the word "church" —*ecclesia*—appear: (Matt. 18:17) "if he refuses to listen, tell it to the church; and if he refuses to listen to the church, let him be to you as a Gentile." Liberal Protestant scholars see in this the introduction of something that, of course, by the time the Gospel took its present form, was definitely in existence. For almost two generations had passed, and the church or *ecclesia* was by this time fairly well established. They point to the utter lack of organization beyond that of the twelve at the time of Jesus' death, and the extreme disorganization which prevailed after his death until Pentecost. They had before this time filled the gap in the ranks of the apostles by choosing Matthias to take Judas' place, but beyond this there is no evidence of formal organization. They were meeting informally together in an upper room where the Pentecostal experience occurred, which seems to have given the impulse to go out and spread the good news of the Gospel. Of course, as necessity required, organization developed; and though at first hardly more than little informal groups meeting in people's homes—Paul writes "to the Church which is in thy house"—gradually it took form, or, perhaps more truly, it took forms which have been perpetuated in the great branches of the church today. Worship seems to have been very simple. The disciples sang a hymn before they left the upper room to go with Jesus to Gethsemane. Jesus apparently took over baptism from John the Baptist, although there is no record in the synoptic Gospels that He Himself ever performed the rite. And on the night that He was betrayed, He had supper with them in the upper room. In the course of the evening, He took bread and wine and gave it to them, bidding them as often as they ate and drank, to do it in remembrance of Him, and Christians have continued ever since some kind of a taking of communion, as we have come to call it. Beyond these things and the fact that He taught them when they pray, to say, "Our Father, who art in Heaven," and that he adjured them to practice prayer in secret, little direction concerning the forms of worship was provided by Jesus. He Himself seems to have participated fully in the Jewish forms of worship current in His day.

Moses, on the other hand, was a master of organization. He took a mass of slaves out of Egypt and led them for forty years or more toward Canaan. Organization was an absolute necessity. And he provided it; I am speaking now of the Moses of the Pentateuch, not necessarily the actual Moses of history.

When plague after plague inflicted upon the Egyptians failed to secure the release of the Hebrews, God resolved to destroy the first-born of all Egyptian families, even to the son of Pharoah. Then He bade Moses prepare the people to leave. With characteristic thoroughness, He gave the people orders as to just what they should do. They should kill a lamb; it must be a yearling and without blemish. Killing it on a certain date, they must sprinkle the two door posts with its blood. It must be roasted and eaten with unleavened bread, and so forth, and this should be done for a memorial throughout all generations forever. Clearly this is the Biblical story of the origin of the Feast of the Passover, and every detail of its observance is prescribed by Moses. Later, at Mt. Sinai, God gave Moses specific directions for the making of the ark of the covenant, and the tabernacle. Not a detail is omitted. The vestments of Aaron and the other priests are described. "It shall have two shoulder pieces attached to its two edges that it may be joined together. And the skilfully woven band upon it to gird it on shall be of the same workmanship and material of gold, blue and purple and scarlet stuff, . . ." (Ex. 28:8) Then, of course, the sacrifices are to be offered in a certain way—the whole Pentateuch is full of just such specific directions concerning the cult.

This was, as liberal scholars believe, the end result of a long period of growth of the cult, but it gets attached to Moses' name as the giver of every bit of it. And it was this minute regimentation of worship that the prophets again and again attacked. Amos crying, "I hate, I despise your feasts, take away from me the noise of your harps, but let justice roll down like the waters" (Amos 5:29-24 *passim*), and Micah (6:8) asking, "What doth the Lord require of you, but to do justly, love mercy and walk humbly with thy God," represent the prophetic revolt against this luxuriant cultic development, a revolt which Jesus, in the prophetic tradition also, shared and pressed with the greatest vigor. "Woe unto you, Scribes and Pharisees, hypocrites! for you tithe mint, and dill and cummin, and have neglected the weightier matters of the law, justice and mercy and faith; . . . . you cleanse the outside of the cup and the plate, but within they are full of extortion and rapacity . . . . you are like whited sepulchres, which without appear beautiful, but are full of dead men's bones." (Matt. 23:23-27.)

Of course, Jesus is here condemning an abuse of the law rather than the Mosaic law itself, for He recognized that within it there were weightier matters which they were neglecting. These, said He, they ought to have done without neglecting the others. (Matt. 23:25) But when religion becomes externalized in a great mass of detailed forms, it seems to become easy to substitute form for the reality behind the form, and men are often content if they be found fulfilling the formal requirements. Jesus' concern was not for the formal, the external, but for the inner heart of man. If this was right, He was apparently content that it externalize itself as it might. The Christian church had to decide early what it would do in this regard. Should it impose upon the new converts the requirements, cultic and legal, of the old Jewish faith? The first Council of the young Church had to deal with the question when Paul made an issue of whether or not non-Jewish converts must be circumcised. The decision was that this was not necessary, thus freeing Christianity to become a world religion rather than a Jewish sect. Christianity has had its own troubles at this precise point: a growing mass of external requirements on the part of the ecclesiastical organization has made it necessary on more than one occasion for some prophetic voice to be raised in protest, and to call the church back to the inner heart of Christian faith.

We have already spoken of the fact that Jesus and Moses were at one in their belief that God was one—at least so far as Israel was concerned—and that He was the guardian of the moral order. I have expressed my own conviction that Moses had not himself reached a fully monotheistic idea of God, but this is a moot question; many believe that he did. But even if Moses had reached monotheism, in a great many other respects his idea of God is far removed from Jesus' idea of Him. First of all, God was associated usually with storm when Moses went up into the mountain to speak with Him. Moses brought the people out of the camp to meet God, says the writer of Exodus, and Mt. Sinai was wrapped in smoke and it quaked mightily. Moses spoke, and God answered him in thunder. (Ex. 19:16-18 *passim.*) And when the people heard the thunder and saw the lightning they cried, "You, Moses, speak to us, but let God not speak to us lest we die." (Ex. 20.18-20.) This idea persists long in Hebrew thought, as in Deborah's song (Judg. 5:4-5), and even the Psalmist speaks of the Lord thundering in the heavens and the earth quaking (Ps. 18: 7-13). It lasts even into the New Testament. John relates that on one occasion a voice spoke out of heaven, and in an aside he remarks, "And the crowd standing by heard it and said, 'it thundered.'" (Jn. 12:27-29.) It may well be that in the Psalms and later, the idea of God as storm may have come to be merely symbolic, but there can be no doubt that in the story of Moses, Yahweh was thought of as a storm God.

Again in the song of Moses, God is called a man of war (Ex. 15:3); Yaweh is his name. He cast Pharoah's army into the sea. He destroyed the enemies that stood in their way. It was he who ordered them to take this people and not that. This tradition of a God of war and battles runs through the whole story of the conquest of Canaan and through the consolidation of the people into a united kingdom under Saul and David. David calls God the God of the armies of Israel, on the eve of his fight with Goliath (I Sam. 17:45). And the psalmist writes of God as "teaching his hands to war" (Ps. 18:34).

God was a jealous God—full of wrath—vengeful and capable of hatred, and seems to have been regarded as parochial or tribal in his interest, concerned with Israel rather than with all mankind. All through the earlier stories of the Hebrew people, reference is made to the gods of other peoples as if they were real gods for those people— lacking seems to be the note of universality.

JESUS AND MOSES

The God of Jesus is, of course, universal, and He is just, merciful, compassionate, and loving. The symbol Jesus chose by which to convey this idea was that of fatherhood. God as Father is not unknown in the Old Testament, but in most cases it is in the sense of progenitor. In the Psalms there is, "Like as a Father pitieth his children"; and in the prophets there is some emphasis on love as well as justice. In Exodus 34:7 God is spoken of as "merciful and gracious, abounding in steadfast love and faithfulness" and in Deuteronomy, which reflects prophetic influence, there is reference to God's love for Israel, but in the New Testament God's universal love and compassion has become a central point of emphasis. In fact, God as interpreted in terms of Jesus' own life and teaching may be said to be the primary difference between Judaism and Christianity.

In respect to their concept of ethics they differ, not as to the ultimate basis, which is God, but in the content read into the term. Certainly, the Mosaic conception of God as vengeful, jealous, and warlike is foreign to Jesus' idea. There is nothing at all in Mosaic teaching to suggest the Sermon on the Mount with its idea of loving one's enemies, forgiving one's persecutors, blessing those that curse one. Indeed, Jesus sets himself sharply over against Mosaic law in his phrase "Ye have heard it said of old time, but I say unto you . . ." Not that the Christian world has accepted the ideals, but it is there cleanly and sharply set over against the older *lex talionis* of Moses. In nothing do they stand in greater contrast.

Of course, Moses lived in a rude age. Lying, deceit, trickery, and cruelty could all be assigned to the character of God even. Many centuries of suffering taught the Hebrews a better way. The prophets each added some new insight concerning the meaning of the good, and Jesus was an inheritor of their contributions. He should, of course, represent a higher conception of ethics than Moses, even on a purely humanistic basis. If, as Christians think, he was the full revelation of God to man, of course his ideals would be higher than that reached by any man, anywhere.

In respect to their beliefs concerning life after death, also, they differ sharply. About all that can be gleaned from a study of the so-called Mosaic writings is that there was some sort of existence after this life. There are two or three references to death customs. In one case, reference is made to offerings to the dead. (Dt. 26:14.) In another it is commanded, "Ye shall not cut yourselves or make any baldness between your eyes for the dead." (Dt. 14:1.) And in still another, "Ye shall not make any cuttings in your flesh for the dead." (Lv. 19:28.) Scholarship is divided as to whether there was an ancestral cult among the early Hebrews. So almost nothing is known concerning what they really thought as to the content of the idea of the after-life. Of course, later Hebrew religion developed a distinct belief in immortality, but it is not, I think, represented as coming from Moses. It takes on added strength and concreteness after the exile, when they were exposed to the Zoroastrian faith, which had a very lively interest in the hereafter and held rather definite ideas of what it was like. Previous to this, it was little, if any, different from the old Babylonian concept, from which they may, indeed, have derived it, since Abraham went out from Ur of the Chaldees.

Of Jesus' conception little need be said, save that it is personally conceived and morally conditioned, as the older

Hebrew idea was not. Jesus gave no clear picture of its content, but affirmed that it was like in spirit to His own. John quotes Him as saying, "I go to prepare a place for you that where I am ye may be also." It was left for Revelation and apocryphal writings to furnish the blueprint of what is often now considered the Christian idea of heaven.

Jesus and Moses also differ as to the manner of their death. Moses goes up into Mt. Nebo, looks across Jordan at the promised land, and dies. "No man knoweth unto this day the place of his burial." He had rounded out 120 years—"his eye was not dim, nor his natural force abated," says the closing chapter of Deuteronomy.

Everyone knows of Jesus' tragic death on the cross, as well as His storied resurrection and ascent into heaven. Jesus and Moses differed greatly in their lives, and even more in their final end.

How have they been dealt with by their followers and successors?

Jesus, of course, was soon thought of as more than human, the divine Son of God, and an elaborate set of Christological theories built up to explain His metaphysical relationship to God, and at the same time to retain His essential humanity. His death and resurrection became the clue to man's redemption, a free giving by God of His Son, as an atonement for the sins of all mankind, according to orthodox Christianity. By all Christians, in one way or another, He is thought of as Savior, the restorer of man's lost relationship to God his Father, whether through Jesus' life and teachings or through His death and resurrection.

What of Moses? We have seen that he has become for Jewish faith the lawgiver *par excellence*. He is the father of all Hebrew law. The Pentateuch, or the Torah, has come to be thought of as the basic thing in Judaism. The writings of the prophets, psalmists, historians, and others serve but to make explicit what is already implicit in the Torah. There is nothing new in them.

Writing of the rabbinical school's idea of Scripture, George F. Moore says, "The notion of progressive revelation was impossible, the revelation to Moses was complete and final: no other prophet should ever make any innovation in the law. The 48 prophets and 7 prophetesses who came after him neither took away anything that was written in the law nor added anything to it except the reading of the roll of Esther. Moses is the fountain head of prophecy in so literal a sense that it is said he uttered all the words of the prophets besides his own. . . all the rest of the books, with no detraction from their divine inspiration and authority, are an authority of the second rank; they repeat, reinforce, amplify and explain the Law, but are never independent of it. Proof texts are often quoted in threes, a verse from the Pentateuch, another from the Prophets and a third from the Hagiographa, not as though the word of the law needed confirmation, but to show how the Scripture emphasizes the lesson by iteration." [5]

So great was the Rabbinic admiration for Moses that some asserted that the creation of heaven and earth were only for his sake. Some of them think that the angels seen ascending and descending the ladder reaching toward heaven in Jacob's dream at Bethel were Moses and Aaron. Many miracles are related as having been performed by Moses in addition to those narrated earlier. When the

[5] George F. Moore, *Judaism* (Cambridge: Harvard University Press, 1927), Vol. I, pp. 239f.

Israelites were about to leave Egypt, Moses wished to carry with them the body of Joseph. Told that it was in the Nile, Moses went to the bank of the river and cried: "Come up, Joseph." At once the coffin appeared and was carried out of Egypt back to the Promised Land. Two leopards guarded the entrance to the palace of the Pharoah, and would allow no one to approach. But as Moses' approach, they played with him like puppies.

He was, according to tradition, distinguished for his strength and manliness; he was ten ells tall and very powerful. His face was surrounded with a halo; yet, withal, he was very modest. The angel of death was, at the end, afraid to take Moses' soul. God Himself descended with Gabriel, Michael, and Zagziel, a former teacher of Moses. Moses then pronounced blessing upon his people, begging their forgiveness for any injury he might have caused them, and assuring them that he would meet them in the resurrection of the dead.

Gabriel arranged the death couch; Michael spread over it a silken cover; his old teacher put a silken pillow under his head. At God's command, Moses closed his eyes and crossed his hands upon his breast, and God took away his soul with a kiss. Then the heavens and the world of stars wept.

A Rabbinic account asserts that, for the love of Israel, Moses went so far to count himself among sinners, and that "he even atoned for all the sins of humanity down to his time, freeing men from the burden of sin." [6] This shows clearly late Christian influence.

In the Hellenistic tradition, the idea appeared that Moses was translated, as seen in the *Assumption of Moses*. Like

---

[6] *Jewish Encyclopedia,* art. *"Moses"* (New York: Funk and Wagnalls, 1909).

the Messiah, he was said to be pre-existent, "prepared before the foundation of the world to be the mediator of God's covenant, and as he was Israel's intercessor before God during life, so is he their intercessor in all the future." [7]

Moore reports one of the rabbis (Simlai) as applying Is. 53:12 specifically to Moses: "I will divide him a portion with the great . . . because he poured out his soul unto death." It is applicable because Moses gave himself over to death, as it is written in Ex. 32:32, "And if thou wilt not forgive their sin, blot me out, I pray, of the book thou hast written." Isaiah 53 goes on to say, "And he was numbered among the transgressors." So was Moses, for he was numbered among those who died in the wilderness. And he "took away the sins of many," refers to Moses, "because he made atonement for the people in the incident of the setting up of the golden calf." [8]

Probably Philo went farther in his exaltation of Moses than any other well-known Jewish figure. E. R. Goodenough says: "He interprets the sacrifice of Moses in Lev. 8:24 as revealing that 'Moses is the perfect man,' because of his sacrifice in which he puts only the beast's breast upon the altar, thus signifying that Moses is beyond any labor with the passions, for he has cut them off altogether; but Aaron is still laboring with the passions." He is still the man, attendant and minister of holy things, and in battle with his lower nature. [9]

Goodenough reports also that Philo, in interpreting the sweetening of the bitter waters at Marah, makes Moses out

---

[7] *Ibid.*

[8] Moore, *op. cit.,* p. 550.

[9] E. R. Goodenough, *By Light, Light* (New Haven: Yale University Press, 1935), p. 217.

as a Savior. "The Israelites would indeed have been lost and returned to Egypt had not the Savior thrown into their lives a bit of wood, a sweetening thing to make them see that toil was sweet." Moses is here acting as the Savior, hierophant for the wanderers.

Again, in the episode of lifting up the brass serpent in the wilderness, Philo represents Moses as Savior. "The serpent is brass," he writes, because this was as near to the golden virtue present in Moses as the people could come. Salvation from pleasure, then, is to look upon the beauty of Sophrosune, the serpent of Moses, and "in seeing this one beholds God himself. Let him look and mark it well." This, says Goodenough, is not casual allegory, as its substantial repetition in another treatise shows. "The mystic looked to the virtue of Moses and in doing so looked upon God. A more definite statement of Moses' power as divine Savior could not be made." He goes on to say a little later: "When Moses stands between God and the people in Dt. 5, it is the Logos mediating for us." [10]

The description of Moses' death, both in the *De Vita Mosis* and elsewhere, strongly suggests to Goodenough that, to Philo, Moses was a God. Philo, he thinks, was a creature of his age and influenced by not only the monotheism of Judaism, but by the Neo-Pythagorean and Platonic traditions in philosophy and also the popular tendency to deify great heroes. How be a monotheist and yet ascribe divinity to persons and principles was a real problem—settled by some in the Christian tradition by thinking of God as surrounded by a body of emanations of his own nature—θεοι but not ὁ θεος.

Philo, he thinks, would theoretically have stood by the

---

[10] *Ibid.*, p. 220.

position that Moses was only one inspired by the Logos, but "Philo did not live by theory," and in his works are to be found—made doubtless under the strain of emotion— "statements about the divinity of Moses which cannot be reconciled with the 'gifted man' passages." [11] For example, he writes, "When God gave *him* (Moses) as a loan to earthly things . . . he did not attach to him any common virtue of a ruler or king . . . rather God ordained him as deity (εἰς θεον) and decreed that all the regions of the body and its dominant mind should be subject and slave to him. 'For I give thee,' He says, 'as a god to Pharaoh.' "

Goodenough adds, "Taken by itself, this passage could only mean that Moses was a deity who was made incarnate by the special decree of God." [12]

In other passages he explains that, from the standpoint of monotheism, Moses was not a God. That is true, but, says Goodenough, "The point to be decided is not whether Philo contradicts his statements of Moses' divinity, but whether he repeats them often enough so that one may assume that it really represents one of his attitudes toward Moses," for he regards Philo as not always consistent.

He sums up in these words: "Was then Moses θεον in Philo's mind? The answer must be yes and no. He is contrasted with God in His pure existence. There was only one Diety in the strict sense for Philo. But if Moses was then contrasted with God, he was quite as sharply contrasted with any man but the patriarch, and with all of them but Isaac, by the fact that his humanity was ultimately meaningless in his almost completely divine nature." [13]

---

[11] *Ibid.*, pp. 223–225 *passim.*
[12] *Ibid.*, p. 225.
[13] *Ibid.*, p. 228.

One even finds this prayer addressed to Moses: "O thou hierophant, though the eyes of our soul are closed because we do not desire to see or cannot do so, still do thou behold us and help us and not cease to anoint us until thou hast initiated us into the hidden meaning of the sacred words and revealed those locked beauties that are invisible to the uninitiated. This it is meet for thee to do."

Writes Goodenough: "This is not an address to one who is dead and gone. Philo sees in Moses an active and present power, and the prayer to Moses for guidance, light, and anointing is precisely such a prayer as Christian mystics have for centuries been addressing to Christ." [14]

The *Jewish Encyclopedia* says that Philo called Moses "the mediator and reconciler of the world." [15]

Nor was Philo alone in his ascription of diety to Moses. The Essenes, says the *Jewish Encyclopedia*, seem to have apotheosized him. "Next to God," writes Josephus, "they honor the name of their legislator, and if anyone blasphemes him he meets with capital punishment. Against such excessive adoration of a human being a reaction set in among the Rabbis, who declared that no man ever ascended into heaven." [16]

This latter, of course, has been the general view of the Jewish people. Especially in their reaction against the deification of Jesus by the Christian Church, and the elaboration of the idea of the Trinity, which they hold is an affront to pure monotheism, they naturally tend to stop in their admiration of the great lawgiver short of deification. Indeed, they are—the more liberal of them—quite likely to stress particularly the human character of Moses.

[14] *Ibid.,* p. 233.
[15] Art., "Moses."
[16] *Ibid.*

A channel he was, through which God revealed his law to man, but a human channel only.

In this belief Christians would warmly accord, for did not St. Paul declare that the law—and Moses was the giver of the law—was a pedagogue to lead men to Christ, whom they regard as the full revelation of God to man?

Jews who stand in the prophetic tradition of Judaism tend increasingly, I think, to put Jesus in that tradition, some even agreeing with the liberal Christians who stumble at the acceptance of the deity of Christ, that he represents the culmination of that prophetic line, even when they cannot go along with the more extreme claims of Christian orthodoxy. But the orthodox Jews continue to see in Moses the basic figure in their faith, the bringer of the Torah, in which everything that is needful for man's salvation has been given. It only needs to be understood and practiced.

10

Jesus and Mohammed

=====□=====

MOHAMMED WAS A LATE COMER ON THE SCENE. LAST OF the founders of what are regarded as the great religions of the world, it was near the end of the sixth century A. D. that he was born. In terms of Christian time-reckoning, he first saw the light about 570 A. D. In Moslem terms, Jesus was born 622 years before Mohammed fled from Mecca to Medina, the event from which all Moslems compute time, as Christians do from the birth of Jesus.

Though surrounded less with legend than that of the birth of most of the founders of the great faiths, his loyal and admiring followers have not wholly refrained from embellishing the story. There was evidently an element of Providence in the preservation of his father from being sacrificed by the prophet's grandfather on one occasion. Abdul Muttalib had one time rashly vowed to sacrifice one of his ten sons. On casting lots, it was his favorite son who was chosen. Distressed, he put up his son's life against 10 camels. Again the son was taken by lot. His father doubled the number of camels—still fate decreed his son's death. At last he staked 100 camels and once again cast lots. This time it was the 100 camels that were chosen to die. Mohammed's father was thus preserved to sire his illustrious son.

Ikbal 'Ali Shah says, " When the prophet was born, extraordinary portents are reported to have been seen in Mecca and beyond. Traditionists have it that fourteen minarets of the mighty palace of Cyrus fell from their proud places; the flame that burned in the holy Persian temple was extinguished; the river Sadah was dried up." [1]

We know rather more about Mohammed than is surely known concerning other religious founders. This is notably true of his sayings, which are preserved in the *Koran*, the sacred book of the Moslems; but there almost nothing is related of the Prophet's life. His name appears but five times in the whole book, which purports to be the recorded revelations to Mohammed from Allah or God, communicated to him through the Angel Gabriel, written down very soon after they were received, and preserved on all sorts of writing materials, such as parchment, the broad bleached shoulder bones of sheep, and so forth. Collection and editing of these are supposed to have been the work of Mohammed's own amanuensis, Zaid, only a few years after his death. It is Moslem dogma that, after the editing of the second edition, under the Caliphate of Othman, all older copies were destroyed, so that there never has been a serious problem of a textual sort in Islam. Modern scholars have discovered that this is by no means so sure; but even so, in comparison with most other scriptures, the *Koran* presents a much simpler problem than that found in relation with any other scripture. It is definitely a one-man book. It was compiled very shortly after the prophet's death, and it soon came to be regarded as so sacred and inviolate that every protection has been thrown around it.

---

[1] Ikbal 'Ali Shah, *Mohamed: the Prophet* (London: Wright & Brown, 1932), p. 80.

Here unmistakably is the major source of the teaching of the Prophet. It has come to be regarded as verbally inspired, very much the way that the Fundamentalist Christians think of their Bible. Most of the chapters begin with the word "Say," which is the equivalent to the Biblical phrase "Thus Saith the Lord." Mohammed, like the Old Testament prophets, spoke forth in the name of God.

But there is a secondary source which supplies us with most of our knowledge of the Prophet himself. This is called the *Hadith*, or the Traditions. Here are preserved what the Companions of the Prophet remembered concerning what the Prophet did and said, beyond what is recorded in the *Koran*. Here, of course, there are thousands of items—many of them quite obviously late and probably the result of the growing veneration for the Prophet. Until now there has been no thoroughgoing scientific study of this mass of material, although beginnings have been made. The major criterion employed by Moslem scholars in judging its contents is that there can be no valid tradition which runs clearly counter to the teachings of the *Koran*. If there is nothing directly opposed to Koranic teaching, then the Tradition may be accepted, provided its lineage as a tradition can be traced back directly to some Companion or early personal follower of the Prophet. Scholars who stand outside the Moslem traditions and have no emotional involvement are inclined to reduce the total number of the authentic traditions to a relatively small number. But it is from this source that most of our information about Mohammed's life must be drawn. Unfortunately, very little of the *Hadith* material has been translated.

Mohammed's birth was that of a normal child, although

portents appeared in the heavens. This was no virgin birth. His family was of the Koreish tribe, and his ancestors had been wealthy and powerful leaders in the community, although at the time of his birth they were in reduced circumstances. His father died before he was born, and he grew up under the protection of his grandfather and certain uncles. Sent, as was customary, to be nursed by a Bedouin woman, his early years were spent, not in Mecca, the city of his birth, but with nomads in the desert. His own mother died when he was but two years old, and as an orphan he was dependent upon his relatives. He thus learned the lore of the desert and became inured to the austere life of the desert wanderers. One of his uncles took him on caravan trips, and he served for years as a kind of commercial traveller following after the caravans to distant places of his world. It was on these many journeys, probably, that he first met the Jews and Christians who gave him such knowledge as he had of Christianity and Judaism. For these faiths—religions of the Book— he had the greatest respect, and he was to base his own faith squarely upon them.

Engaged finally by a wealthy Meccan widow as her caravan manager, he proved so successful, and at the same time so attractive to his employer, Khadijah, that she sought his hand in marriage. It was a happy union, although she was 15 years his senior, and to her good sense and balance he owed a great deal. So long as she lived, he took no other wife, although polyamy was the accepted pattern of his time.

With the freedom which his new position gave him, Mohammed was able to give free reign to his mystical tendency, which a busy commercial life as an employee had not permitted him to indulge. But it can hardly be thought that now for the first time this tendency appeared. He began to spend long hours in meditation in a cave in Mt. Hira, some distance out of Mecca. Here he sometimes fell into a trance and heard a voice speaking to him. He could not understand it, and when ordered to speak in the name of Allah, he distrusted himself. Only when encouraged by his loyal and devoted wife did he venture to believe that this might be his call to be a prophet of God. Once convinced of his calling, he began to preach in the name of Allah to his circle of friends. Few listened to him and believed. But some did. Little by little, he grew bolder and spoke to larger circles. He got persecution for his trouble. Particularly, his denunciation of the worship of many Gods instead of the one Allah, and of the idolatrous practices of the people, stirred the anger of those who profited from the coming of numerous pilgrims yearly to worship at the Meccan Shrine: the Kaaba, with its 360 various figures of different gods. The pressure became so heavy that some of his followers sought sanctuary in Abyssinia, and eventually he accepted the invitation to remove to Medina, where in the course of time he became ruler, and thence set out on a career of conquest which brought most of Arabia under his control before his early death. This flight, or *hegira*, as it is called, took place in 622 A. D. It marks the turn in Mohammed's fortunes and is regarded as the watershed in history from which both past and future happenings in the world are dated by Moslems.

For ten years Mohammed lived in Medina opposed at first by part of the inhabitants but finally accepted as effective ruler. During these years of personal rule, he continued to pour out revelations vouchsafed to him from

Allah, which were to furnish for all time the basis of almost every phase of Moslem life, from conduct in the home, to the management of the entire government. No longer the mystic in the cave, alone with God, but now a ruler of men, cumbered with the cares and responsibility of state, and even at times the leader of battles against the infidels, the prophet, by his every utterance and act, set precedents which the faithful all over the world still follow meticulously, believing that it is the will of Allah that they do.

After only ten years at Medina, the Prophet died and was buried beneath the roof of Aisha, his favorite young wife—but not before his enemies in Mecca had been subdued and he had returned in honor to make his last pilgrimage to the sacred city, walk seven times around the Kaaba, drink from the sacred well, and perform the other acts which pilgrims had long practiced before Mohammed appeared. But now he cleansed the Kaaba of the hateful images of the old Arabian gods and directed that henceforth all these sacred acts were duties to Allah, sole God, of whom Mohammed was Prophet.

There was nothing unusual about his death. He fell ill, suffered from a high fever, rallied once or twice, so that it appeared for a time that he might recover. He even returned to lead the prayers in the mosque once more. He was heard to pray, "O Lord, I beseech thee assist me in the agonies of death. . . . O Gabriel, come close to me, close to me." Then finally, "O Lord, grant me pardon and join me to the companionship on high. O Allah, be it so among all the glorious associates in paradise." Then he was gone.

Jesus and Mohammed differed at many points. Superficially, we may note first that there was comparatively little of the miraculous about Mohammed's life. But there was some. The famous Night Journey is familiar to every Moslem, whereby Mohammed was caught up and borne first to Jerusalem, where he met with Abraham, Moses, Jesus, and the others, and was afterwards taken through successive heavens to the highest, before he was returned to his couch. This famous journey bears some likeness to the transfiguration experience of Jesus. It is told briefly without detail in the *Koran*, but devotion has elaborated it into a colorful, fascinating story told and retold around a thousand caravan fires in the desert. One account of it tells how in the fifth heaven he saw but the veiled face of Allah, covered over with 20,000 veils, yet the glory which radiated from that face was greater than fifty thousand sunrises.[2] On the right hand of the throne of God he saw inscribed the Creed of Islam, "There is no God but Allah, and Mohammed is his Messenger."

It is not so stated in the *Koran*, but tradition clearly emphasizes the miraculous events which occurred sometimes in the battles in which Mohammed fought. One story is this: The first critical battle of Badr was under way. Mohammed was watching it. He become so excited that he lost consciousness. Coming to in a spirit or exaltation, he is said to have picked up a handful of dust and flung it in the direction of the enemy, crying: "May confusion light upon their faces." So saying he mounted a horse and charged the enemy. Some say that at this point a host of angels with Gabriel at their head joined Mohammed and his fighting forces. Actually, it is said that a violent sandstorm sprang up suddenly and blinded the enemy. Al-

---

[2] R. V. C. Bodley, *The Messenger*, p. 114. Copyright, 1946, by R. V. C. Bodley. Reprinted by permission of Doubleday & Company, Inc.

ready weary and thirsty, they were thrown into confusion, and, although greatly outnumbering the Moslems, they fled before them and a great victory was won for Allah and his Prophet. It was a crucial turning point in the career of Mohammed.[3]

Jesus had but a short ministry—something between a year and a half and three years. Mohammed's Meccan ministry was ten years, and he had a full decade of active leadership in Medina. Jesus' was largely a teaching and preaching ministry; that of Mohammed was preaching—particularly during the first ten years—but not merely of preaching and leading the mosque worship. During his Medina period he was also a political figure, engaged in the practical management of a city, as well as in the organization of armies and even the conduct of military expeditions. He was at once lawmaker and judge. The whole basis of Moslem jurisprudence is to be found in the way Mohammed personally dealt with specific cases that were brought to him for settlement.

Again, somewhat superficially, these men differed in their family relationships. Jesus never married and, of course, knew nothing of fatherhood—except vicariously, if it be true, as tradition has it, that he was the support of the family in Nazareth after the death of Joseph. Mohammed, on the other hand, was a family man. He was married first to Khadijah, with whom he lived monogamously for some 15 years and by whom he had six children. After her death, he remained a widower for some time, then married successively 11 wives—most of them widows, some of them certainly not young and attractive. Only three of them probably could be said to have been

---

[3] *Ibid.*, pp. 159–160.

notable for their feminine charm. All this was quite in
the spirit of the times and the place in which Mohammed
lived. There was no limit to the number of wives a man
might have in Arabia until Mohammed placed a limit of
four upon his followers. That he himself overstepped the
limit, justifying it by a special revelation in his own case,
has been a perennial source of criticism by the Christian
world, which has been none too friendly to the Arabian
prophet. Attack by enemies of Islam at this point has led
Moslem apologists to concentrate their efforts at explanation here, and all kinds of suggestions have been made. The
effort has been made to show that, so far from proving
Mohammed's passion for women, it was rather the result
of his benevolence that he was so much married. Certainly there is in the *Koran* itself clear evidence that the
domestic arrangements of the Prophet were not always
conducive to spiritual calm. But to provide protection for
women whose husbands had fallen in the Holy cause, he
was willing sometimes to bring them into the shelter of
his own household. Also, some marriages were for the
purpose of cementing relationships between Mohammed
and some of his followers. Thus, Aisha, his youngest and
favorite wife, was the daughter of Abu Bekr, who was to
be his successor as head of the faith. One gets the impression that a good deal too much stress has been placed at
this point by non-Moslems. Polygamy, if not permissible
now, concurrently, at any rate, was clearly the pattern of
his age and country. It would have been very remarkable
had he risen above it. Moslem apologists have probably
been right, as well as fairly successful, in showing what
improvements Mohammed by his teaching and practice
made in the general treatment of women in Arabia. He

outlawed female infanticide, then a common practice. He gave women legal rights to the independent ownership of property, even though married, which women in some so-called Christian European countries do not even yet enjoy. And in certain passages in the *Koran*, he unquestionably laid the basis for a sense of individual dignity and worth on the part of women which, once recognized and practiced as it is coming to be recognized in some Moslem lands today, augurs well for the future of Islam's womanhood. Some even profess to find a profound basis for monogamy in the Prophet's dictum that one must love and treat equally the women he marries. Since this is manifestly impossible, monogamy is clearly indicated.

Here is obviously a sharp difference between the two founders. Jesus says little about marriage. He discourages, if, as part of the Christian world firmly holds, He does not completely disallow divorce and, certainly, remarriage. He finds in the family relationship the very language which He uses to express the relationship of man and God. God is Father and man is a child of God—a conception quite foreign to Islam, where the relationship is better expressed in terms of ruler and subject, but of this more later.

Again, Mohammed apparently never thought of himself as other than a prophet. On more than one occasion, he asserted this categorically. In the third surah, it is recorded: "Mohammed is no more than an apostle; other apostles have already passed away before him. If he die, therefore, or be slain, will ye turn on your heels?" We shall see later that this has not always been accepted by all his followers, but it seems clearly to have been the Prophet's own conception of himself.

There is good evidence, both in the *Koran* and in the

Traditions, that he thought of himself as the fulfillment of Biblical prophecy in relation to the Jews of Arabia. Apparently he hoped to be accepted by them as the one whom they were expecting to come. And their failure to recognize him as such is probably the cause of his turning against them. What Jesus thought of Himself and His peculiar relationship to God has been a matter of disagreement among Christians. Did Jesus ever unequivocally assert a more-than-human character? Some say that He did, even in the synoptics; while in the Gospel of John it seems to them abundantly clear that He regarded Himself as divine. "I and the Father are One." "He that hath seen me hath seen the Father," so the record goes. Most orthodox Christians hold that He consciously knew of and proclaimed His divinity—certainly toward the close of His brief earthly ministry. If He did, He certainly at this point differs sharply from Mohammed. What those who came afterward have come to think of the two, we shall see a little later.

The two men differed sharply in their attitudes toward their enemies. Mohammed clearly followed the old pattern of an eye for an eye and a tooth for a tooth. For him, Jesus' saying: "but I say unto you, love your enemies" was as unacceptable as it is to much of the world today, which regards Him as a hopeless dreamer and idealist. Enemies were to be attacked and subdued or destroyed by violence. Turning the other cheek was not for Mohammed. He was persecuted in the early days in Mecca, and he bore it nobly without yielding his principles, except once when, under very severe pressure, he allowed that the sisters of Allah be accorded worship. But it was only a passing weakness. Quickly he withdrew the concession and returned to his rigid monotheistic teaching that Allah alone was worthy of worship. But there was no prayer of forgiveness for his persecutors.

An admirer of Mohammed, writing of the battle of Badr, relates the story of the slaying of Abu Johl, leader of the Koreishites. When the slayer bore the severed head of the enemy to Mohammed, he says, "Mohammed looked at the gory trophy in ecstasy; withdrawing from the fighting he dismounted and prostrated himself. 'There is no God but Allah,' he cried. 'Abu Johl has been punished as shall be punished all enemies of Allah.' " [4]

The same writer, basing his statements doubtless on the Traditions rather than the *Koran* itself, tells of a woman poetess who wrote a variety of verses lampooning Mohammed. One night, a blind Moslem, deeply resentful of the insults to the Prophet, crept into the women's tent and plunged his sword into her breast, killing her. Addressing the congregation in the mosque next day, Mohammed is reported as saying; "If ye desire to see a man who hath assisted the Lord and his Messenger, look ye here."

Let it be confessed that this may not be a true report; nevertheless, it has been preserved across the centuries as evidently not foreign to the spirit of the Prophet. Certainly no such traditions exist concerning Jesus.

It is true, too, that the Christian world has probably overstressed the element of force and violence employed by Mohammed and his followers in spreading the Prophet's teaching. It is also true that Christian armies have marched and pillaged and destroyed. But Jesus Himself is never accused of having engaged in any act of violence beyond

[4] *Ibid.*, p. 160.

that of driving the money changers out of the temple, crying "You have made my father's house a den of thieves and robbers." He never led an army. He never in any word encouraged men to fight in his cause.

And when Christians today take up arms against their fellows, it is always with some sense of guilt, a feeling that they somehow have to justify their acts in the face of what Jesus taught and what He practiced. Jesus has been put in *khaki* in wartime and even in peace, but never quite without apology or a gesture of admiration at least for the Sermon on the Mount, which is generally accepted as the very heart of His teaching.

Bodley, without citing his source, reports Mohammed as declaring: "A drop of blood shed in the cause of God, a night spent in arms, is of more avail than two months of fasting and prayer. Whoever falls in battle, his sins shall be forgiven. At the Day of Judgment, his wounds shall be resplendent in vermillion and odoriferous as musk, and the loss of his limbs shall be supplied by wings of angels and cherubims." [5]

On one occasion, the Jews had traitorously sought to betray the Moslems when they were besieged in Medina. When the Jews in turn had been beseiged and had been subdued, they were brought before Mohammed. They begged that someone who would be impartial be designated to arbitrate their fate, agreeing to accept without question his decision. Mohammed agreed, and they named one Saad ibn Muad. His judgment was, "that the men be put to death, the women and children sold into slavery, and the spoil be divided among the Moslem soldiery." The Jews could not believe their ears, and fell on their knees

---

[5] *Ibid.*, p. 157, *cf.* The Koran, Sura 47.

pleading for mercy. But at the orders of Mohammed, the women and children were led off in one direction, the men in the other, and the sentence carried out quite literally, Mohammed in no way interfering. A western Moslem apologist points out that this was precisely the fate meted out to enemies of the Hebrews, quoting Dt. 20: "And when the Lord hath delivered the city into their hands, thou shalt smite every male thereof with the edge of the sword. But the women and the little ones, and the cattle, and all that is in the city, even all the spoil thereof, shalt thou take unto thyself." But no justification for such a deed could be found in the Gospel, or, indeed, in the whole New Testament. Jesus specifically set aside such ancient law and practice when he said: "Ye have heard it said of old time . . . but I say unto you." The aforesaid western writer defends the Prophet's attitude, saying, "Had he been weak, had he allowed treachery to go unpunished, Islam would never have survived. This massacre of Hebrews was drastic, but not original in religious history. From a Moslem point of view, it was justified." Precisely, but not from Jesus' point of view. That was one of the great differences between them. Maybe Mohammed was right; possibly, Jesus was wrong. By and large, the world has followed Mohammed in this respect rather than Jesus. But that does not establish the truth of his views. Brought to the brink of destruction in this atomic age by a logical following-out of this philosophy, not a few are wondering if indeed practical good sense does not lie rather in the law of love, which Jesus taught and exemplified in His own personal life.

It is not a little strange, therefore, to discover among the Traditions an occasional statement that does approximate the Sermon on the Mount. "Say not, if people do good to us, we will do good to them, and if people oppress you, we will oppress them; but resolve that if people do good to you, you will do good to them, and if they oppress you, oppress them not again." [6]

Also, along with his emphasis on military powers, it is pleasant to reflect that he did now and again prove forgiving to enemies—as, for example, when on entering Mecca triumphantly after years of fighting with the Koreishites, on the whole, when they submitted, he forgave them, when he might have put them to the sword.

At no point were Mohammed and Jesus farther apart than in their conceptions of God. Both, of course, believed in one God, who was to be worshipped non-idolatrously. But the nature of God, as reflected in their teachings, is very different. It is easy to oversimplify their ideas and to represent the two founders as believing only this or that about God. It is important to note that in neither case are we dealing with a systematic theologian. These men were primarily experiencers of God rather than theologians, reflecting upon and attempting to explain God in rational terms. Both undoubtedly felt that they were in direct communication with God in a special way, that God was speaking through them, Jesus undoubtedly felt at times awe and reverence in the presence of God, as Mohammed did, but the dominant emphasis in His thought about God was not that. Jesus seems to have thought of God in intimately personal terms. To be sure, at times God loomed as Judge in Jesus' thought, and He pronounced judgment upon sinful, rebellious man in God's

---

[6] Stanley Lane-Poole, *The Speeches and Table-Talk of the Prophet Mohammed* (London: Macmillan & Co., Ltd., 1905), p. 147.

name. But that was not a primary note in His teaching. God was the Father who loved and sought the reconciliation of His disobedient and wayward children. Jesus thought of Himself as sent by God, commissioned to proclaim the Kingdom of God, to invite man to prepare for its coming. In His own words He had come, obviously called by God, to seek and to save that which was lost. The well had no need of a physician, but there were many sick who needed His ministry, and He had come to minister to them in God's name. He was the instrument for a forthreaching God who took the initiative in seeking to restore the broken relationship of love and obedience which was the normal one between God the Father and His children. As previously indicated, He took the moralized family relationship as the symbol of the true relationship between God and man. He made love the primary quality of the divine life, defining God essentially as love itself. Granting that there were other elements in His total teaching, can it be denied that this is central in His gospel?

Such was certainly not the major emphasis of the Arabian prophet. There are not lacking elements of mercy and compassion in Allah. It is certainly not without significance that all but one of the 114 Surahs in the *Koran* opens with this rubric known as the *Bismillah*: "In the name of God, the merciful and the compassionate." But this may be only a formal statement essentially ritualistic in character. Certainly there is a more insistent element of judgment in the *Koran* than in the Gospels. "Woe unto you, unbelievers," occurs with a frequency not found in Jesus' preaching. Nor is the father-son relationship at all present in the *Koran*. If one were to try to find one phrase which would more properly express the true relationship, it would be that of sovereign and subject rather than father and son.

One scholar, seeking to get at the primary emphasis in the *Koran*, which, of course, represents Mohammed's thought—not that of later theologians—fixes upon power as the chief point of emphasis. He analyzes the 99 beautiful names of Allah, and finds an overwhelming percentage of them to convey some aspect of power. It may be significant that he quite neglected to take into account the frequency with which they occur in the *Koran*. Taking this into account—for example, the instant recurrences of the phrase "The merciful and compassionate," in the *Bismillah*—might considerably alter the picture.

Another Christian scholar [7] is of a different opinion. There is doubtless an emphasis upon power, he thinks; but more accurately, "the chief characteristic of the Islamic conception of God is His Absolute will: Allah does as he wills." Man may never call his actions in question, "since Allah is far above any law or necessity. He is the absolute Ruler." How far this was the genuine teaching of Mohammed himself or the elaboration of generations of systematic theologians it is not easy to say. Mohammed did say in the *Koran*, "Whom he will, he leadeth astray." There is undoubtedly a Koranic basis for the doctrine of the decrees, the election of some to salvation and some to destruction. If it be said that this, too, occurs in Christianity—indeed, it has been generally believed that Augustine's doctrine of the decrees may have influenced Mohammed—and that it is rooted in the New Testament, it is still true that it is found in Paul, not in the Gospels, and

---

[7] L. Levonian, *Studies in the Relationship of Islam and Christianity* (London: George Allen & Unwin, Ltd., 1940), p. 88.

that one would be hard put to it to find a satisfactory basis for such a doctrine in any recorded word of Jesus.

I confess that, in a reading of the *Koran*, I find an alternation of emphasis. God is sovereign—of that there can be no doubt. He is judge, and His prophet pronounces terrible judgment upon unbelievers at times. But there are other times when a note of tenderness creeps in. Men are besought to believe in Him, with clear implication that they are free to do so or not, as they will. Certainly, there is a warm, devotional attitude on the part of some Moslems, and the Sufi-mystics have produced a literature of prayer that has very much the ring of the greater Christian mystics' prayers. They have undoubtedly been nurtured on this aspect of Mohammed's teaching. It is not wholly one-sided; yet it would be fair, I think, to say that the dominant emphasis has been on the aspect of power—or will, and perhaps even justice, as in the case of the Hebrews. It certainly was not upon love, where Jesus seems to have placed it. At this point they differ substantially.

If Jesus and Mohammed differ in important respects, they are, on the other hand, very much alike in other ways. Both were unquestionably prophets. Jesus may have been more than a prophet—much more—as orthodox Christianity has always insisted; but at the very lowest Christological level, He was certainly prophet. When Jesus asked His disciples who men thought He was, they replied, "Some say you are Moses; some Elias; some John the Baptist." That is, a prophet. His whole ministry proclaims that He belonged to the prophetic line. Every act was in the prophetic strain. He was an innovator; He was not bound rigidly to the past; He was free to criticize formerly accepted ideas and practices. His attitude toward the cult of His day was strikingly like that of His great predecessors. He saw the emptiness of mere form and ritual, and demanded sincerity of heart, a regard for spiritual values, a concern for the inside of the cup—not merely the outside. All this is true to the prophetic pattern, however much further He may be thought to have gone. He put Himself squarely among the prophets and anticipated for Himself the normal fate of the prophets in His remark, "They stoned the prophets." He is accepted increasingly in the prophetic role in Modern Judaism and even given the pre-eminence among the whole galaxy of Hebrew prophets by some, even when they deny Him the character of divinity accepted by most Christians. Jesus was certainly a prophet.

That was, of course, the announced and accepted role of Mohammed, who never claimed to be anything more. Enough for him to consider himself, as he seems to have done, and as his followers unmistakably do, as the seal of all prophecy. He gladly recognized Jesus as among the prophets, and his followers generally are willing to put Him high on the list of prophets—indeed, just beneath the name of the Prophet of Allah.

Both were much given to prayer and meditation. We have already spoken of the extended periods of solitude which Mohammed enjoyed in a cave on Mt. Hira, where he seems to have gotten his call. Jesus' frequent excursions into the mountains or off to the lakeside where He could have uninterrupted communion with His father are abundantly familiar. He lived by prayer and communion with God. Prayer was a never-failing source of strength to Him. Both knew themselves dependent upon this spiritual refreshment and guidance from God. Both were mystics, with a practical bent as well. This clearly appears in the history of the developing movements to which they gave rise.

Both were reformers. Of course, this was a part of their common prophetic function. Jesus found Himself in a period of religious degeneracy, relatively speaking. There was an overwhelming emphasis upon the formal aspects of religion. Pharisees were meticulously tithing "mint and anise and cummin," neglecting the weightier matters of the law.

Their reforming labors took different directions; Mohammed chose the way of authority, creating an instrument of power in government, a theocracy. Jesus took the way of teaching and winning man's loyalty to Himself and to His ideas. Mohammed, it is true, said, "There is no compulsion in religion," and was tolerant especially of Jews and Christians, "people of the Book"; but he did assess heavier taxation upon them if they continued in their own faith. This is, of course, a mild type of coercion, but it did serve to bring many, whose Jewish or Christian convictions lay very near the surface, into the fold of Islam. There was no coercion at all in the teaching of Jesus, unless it might be that of fear of the judgment, which, it must be admitted, He used in much the same manner, although I should say, in less degree, than the Arabian prophet. Other coercion there was none in Jesus' ministry. Mohammed, forsaking to some degree his prophetic functions, becomes a civil magistrate. He makes laws of a detailed sort to fit almost every contingency. Jesus gave general principles, leaving it to men's own intelligence and good will to find a practical way of working out those principles in individual and social life.

Both prophets were deeply concerned about the social problems of their time. Both were champions of social justice. It has often been asserted that early Islam was a type of socialism. It is today being stressed by Communists that both they and Islam are seeking the realization of the same social ends. Communism claims to have the machinery for achieving those ideals in practice, if only Moslems will embrace their Communistic faith.

Both prophets stressed brotherhood, disregarded race and class, and were concerned that men live together amicably and co-operatively. By and large, Islam has been able to maintain a brotherly relationship between races and classes within the Islamic fold. They have, Christians sometimes charge, limited this attitude of brotherhood to those who embrace the faith of the Prophet. But whether this could properly be asserted of the Prophet himself is not so clear. Part of the ease with which Islam reaches the dark folk of Africa is due to their general reputation in respect to race, as over against that of white European Christians.

Both incurred the wrath of the defenders of the status quo of their day. Both were persecuted, and both for very much the same reasons. Mohammed was able finally to gain the upper hand through political organizations and military power, and so to overcome his enemies. Jesus died after a short ministry, refusing to try to operate through the instruments of political power, although some urged it upon Him. He died upon the cross in apparent defeat and disgrace. Mohammed escaped death and rose to a triumphant place of power.

If we have emphasized these two founders' different beliefs in God, let it be said that there is a large area of agreement even here. Both believed in and probably got from the same source—the religion of the Hebrews—the oneness of God. Jesus was a thorough Jew in this respect. He must, as a worshipping Jew, have repeated times without number the Shema: "Hear, O Israel. The Lord our God is one Lord." This appears in the Moslem Creed as "There is no God but Allah." They differed concerning the nature and character of God, but not as to His unity. Jesus, of course, knew nothing of the Trinity, which later Christianity adopted as the orthodox view of the total nature of God, though it was upon His teaching and person that the doctrine was finally erected. Mohammed's doctrine of God is in many ways essentially that of Unitarian Christianity or Judaism, but with different overtones.

Both believed in God as the ultimate moral authority in the universe. While they differed in specific definition of that morality, it is God in both cases who is guarantor of the moral order of the world. In Jesus, Christians find their definition of the moral character of God in personal terms and in terms of His teaching. God is, in His moral and spiritual nature, like Jesus. Mohammed sets forth, in his revelations from Allah in the *Koran*, and in his sayings and acts which are preserved in the Traditions, the practical moral demands which God makes upon his creatures.

Because both believe in a moral order in the universe, both believe in God's judgments upon man and are quite in agreement in the principle of retribution, the belief that God rewards and God punishes. Again, they differ in specific content of the judgment, but both are certain that man, both individually and collectively, is held morally responsible by God for his acts.

Further, both believed and taught that retribution is not completely confined to this life. Life goes on beyond the grave; and in the after-life, man experiences the continuing judgment of God. Again details differ, but the faith of both in an ongoing life in which retribution, positive or negative, finds its fulfillment is unmistakable.

Both apparently held that man is free to make his choice as to whether he will believe in or follow their teachings. In the case of Islam, this hardly seems consistent with the doctrine of the decrees attributed to the Mohammed. This may only mean, as above indicated, that Mohammed was not a systematic thinker; but neither was Jesus. In both faiths, later theologians have elaborated contradictory systems of belief which no amount of discussion can bring into agreement.

From all these considerations, it is clear that Mohammed and Jesus have a great deal in common, as well as points of difference.

How have their later followers thought of Jesus and Mohammed? My readers are, of course, familiar with what has happened in the case of Jesus. First regarded undoubtedly as a prophet, He early came to be thought of as more than human. It is not so clear in the Synoptic Gospels, particularly if one takes the modern critical view of them. Was the great confession a genuine report of what was said in Jesus' own time, or is it a reflection of a later stage of thought? But in the gospel of John, Jesus has already grown beyond the merely human prophetic figure, such as that of Mohammed. He is identified with the word that was in the beginning, the word that was with God, the word that was God, but was "made flesh and dwelt among us (and we beheld his glory, the glory as of the only begotten of the Father), full of grace and truth." (Jn. 1:14.)

In Paul, the Trinitarian formula appears repeatedly in his apostolic benediction, although perhaps the full implication of later Trinitarian thought may not have been his, as set forth in the Athanasian Creed, "very God of very God."

The Christian world has differed at one time or another all the way from the view of His complete humanity through every grade of mixture of the human and divine in His nature, to that highest of all Christologies which makes Him very God, of very God. The generally orthodox view has tended toward the higher Christology, but always with dissenting liberal minorities emphasizing and re-emphasizing the human element in His nature. Modern Unitarianism is but the latest formal statement of this perennial view. All, however, are in agreement that in Him God has given man his highest revelation of Himself. All are agreed that in some unique sense Jesus is the clue to man's salvation, whether through some kind of supernatural atonement, or through showing men the way to a right relationship with God. For some, it is through Jesus' death; for others, it is pre-eminently through His life and teaching that He becomes in a real sense man's Savior.

How have Moslems thought of their Prophet? At the orthodox level, if one may use the majority sect of the Sunnites as normative in Islam, the generally accepted belief is that he was in no sense divine, but only a prophet of Allah. Indeed, he is but one of the prophets of God. Greatest, yes, undoubtedly, but they have generally been content to accept his own estimate of himself, as only a messenger or prophet of Allah. Nor have they any objection to honoring Jesus, as, next to Mohammed, the greatest of the prophetic line.

But, despite this general affirmation of the utter humanity of Mohammed, there has developed a theological concept of prophethood, and particularly of Mohammed's prophethood, which looks certainly in the direction of attributing a more than human nature to their prophet. At least, they are attributes which are applied by theologians to Jesus as a means of emphasizing His divinity.

For example, fairly early there developed a disposition to attribute to Mohammed miraculous powers—one of the proofs of Jesus' divinity among the Orthodox Christians. This, quite in spite of the Prophet's own specific disclaimer that he was a worker of miracles. Undoubtedly it was the answer of Moslems to Christian claims to the superiority of Jesus over Mohammed. In the tenth century, in the *Apology of Al Kindi*, there appeared miracle stories of the ox and the wolf speaking in confirmation of Mohammed's prophethood; of a tree which moved toward him on one occasion; of a shoulder of goat's flesh which warned him that it had been poisoned; of the production of much needed water to satisfy the thirst of his followers. Likewise, he is reported to have healed a grievous wound on the leg of one of his followers at the battle of Kharba by breathing upon it, and there is a report later of healings imparted by the Prophet's clothing, reminiscent of Mk. 5: 30, and Acts 19:12. [8] The same writer (Vol. 2, p. 129) cites the denial by An Nazzam of the miracle of the splitting of the moon; the pebbles praising Mohammed, and water being produced from the fingers of the Prophet,

---

[8] J. H. Sweetman, *Islam and Christian Theology* (London: Lutterworth Press, 1946), Vol. I, p. 36.

thus furnishing additional evidence of miracles attributed to Mohammed and at the same time indicating a reluctance on the part of the apologist An Nazzam to accept the belief in the Prophet as a worker of miracles.

Then there has developed among Moslems a doctrine of the sinlessness of the Prophet—again an attribute of Jesus, according to Christian theologians. This Christian doctrine sets Jesus above the human level, as described by the Pauline declaration: "All have sinned and come short of the Glory of God" (Rm. 3:33), or the Old Testament dictum, "for there is no man that sinneth not" (2 Chron. 6:36).

Sweetman writes: "The impeccability of the prophet cannot be said to have much support from the Qur'an, but in the early exposition of the doctrine (of prophets) in Islam, this tenet is set in the very forefront. By the time of Al Ashari, the dogma is fixed as orthodox that, after assuming the office, it is not possible for the prophet to commit any deadly or even minor sins. The assertion of the sinlessness of Christ was met by the doctrine of the sinlessness of the prophets." [9] And Duncan B. MacDonald, in *Aspects of Islam*, declares categorically, "Islam holds at the present time a fixed doctrine of the sinlessness of its Prophet." [10]

Particularly in the modern period, among Sectarian Moslems at least, there is a definite tendency to idealize the prophet and to find in him an exemplar very much as Christians have found in Christ.

Perhaps the doctrine of the Perfect Man, with which— at least among some of the Sufis—Mohammed was iden-

[9] *Ibid.*, Vol. II, p. 128.

[10] Duncan B. MacDonald, *The Religious Attitude and Life in Islam* (Chicago: University of Chicago Press, 1909).

tified, comes closest to making him more than human. A Sufi in the fourteenth century seems clearly to identify him with the Logos. (Abdul-Karim al Jili, born in 1365 A. D.) He holds, so Levonian says, "That in every age Perfect Men are the outward expression of the essence of Mohammed." [11]

MacDonald cites a Tradition, which he believes is not doubted by any Orthodox Moslem, that makes Allah say: "Had it not been for thee (Mohammed), I had not created the world." That is, says MacDonald, Mohammed or the determination to create Mohammed had been there from the beginning of the world, and the worlds were created and exist only for his sake." [12] Another Tradition has Mohammed declare: "I was a prophet when Adam was between clay and water," that is, before he was really created. Still another calls Mohammed "The first created, and the last to rise in the resurrection."

The great Al-Ghazali discusses the matter thus: "Mohammed said, 'I am the first of the prophets by creation, and the last by mission.' Here, however, creation means predestination, not literal creation, because, before his mother conceived him he was not existent and created. . . . Mohammed was a prophet by predestination, before the creation of Adam . . . know that God predestines first, and then creates or brings into being." [13]

Among the theologians one discovers a developed idea of a pre-existent "Light of Mohammed." This has appeared in all the prophets from Adam to Jesus and, at last, in the Arabian Prophet. The Sufis hold that this light manifests itself in the saints. One of the Sufis, Rayazid

---

[11] Levonian, op. cit., p. 55.
[12] MacDonald, op. cit., p. 97.
[13] Quoted by Levonian, op. cit., p. 55.

Bistami, expresses the idea thus: "That which the prophets have may be compared to a skin containing honey. A single drop trickles from it and that drop is the portion of the saints, while to our Prophet, on whom be peace— belongs all the honey in the skin." [14]

Perhaps in keeping with this view, or perhaps causing the view, was the development of the tradition that Ikbal 'Ali Shah writes of Mohammed's childhood among the Bedouins: "Such manifestations their eyes had never seen, such light playing about the boy." [15] Another tradition takes this form: "Allah created in the beginning of all things the light of Mohammed; from a portion of it he then created his throne; from another portion the lower worlds; . . . from another portion the tablets upon which the decrees of destiny were written; and from another, preserved for the purpose, came the Prophet himself." [16]

It is among the Shiahs that this doctrine has found its greatest development. It is the basis of their doctrine of the Imamate which distinguishes the group sharply from the major Sunnite sect. This Divine Light, a part of God, manifests itself in the Imam, and at his death is passed on to his successor. Sometimes this is by birth, passing from father to son. Thus, Ali Khan, the much-married playboy, may one day receive and manifest the Light which now resides in the Aga Khan, head of the Ismaili sect. Others regard it as passing to another by sudden illumination. In the case of Ali, cousin and son-in-law of Mohammed, it is believed by the Shiahs to have passed from Mohammed through the family line, rather than to Abu Bekr or Omar

[14] *Ibid.*, p. 56.
[15] Ikbal, 'Ali Shah, op. cit., p. 85.
[16] Quoted by MacDonald, *op. cit.*, p. 99.

or Othman and the Summite Caliphs. It is undoubtedly this which passed on to Hasan and Husain, the sons of Ali, who suffered a martyr's death. The anniversary of the death of the latter, observed at Kerbala annually by the Shiahs, is the point at which the Shiahs come closest of all the Moslems to a deification—not of Mohammed himself, but of Ali and his sons. The belief in them and the succeeding Imams as intercessors for the believers before Allah looks in the same direction. This belief is utterly rejected by the Sunnis.

The rigid monotheistic and non-idolatrous nature of Islam has been preserved at the upper levels of Islam; but not at the popular level. Here Islam like Christianity and other faiths has not escaped crasser forms of expression. It was in reaction to the lush growth of the veneration of saints, manifested in pilgrimages to the tombs of the Saints, and pre-eminently to that of Mohammed at Medina, and of other beliefs and practices, such as the popular animistic beliefs in the *djinn* or genii, that the Islamic puritan revolt of the Wahabis took place in the early nineteenth century.

So Jesus and Mohammed stand side by side. It will not do for Christians to belittle the Prophet. No one could start a religion with the vigor, driving power, and staying qualities which Islam has, unless there was a great deal of truth in it. From the viewpoint of the Christian, doubtless Mohammed, even at his best, will seem to be only a belated Hebrew Prophet, a throwback from the standpoint of the insight which Jesus brought into the nature of God and the world and man. But it will be a mistake if the Christian world arrogantly seeks to impose its more highly developed faith upon the Moslems. Many a Moslem in our own day is, let it be said, essentially a Unitarian Christian in his attitude toward Jesus. Some Moslems I have known personally have attained to a quality of life which the best of Christians might well covet. Were it not better to recognize in them fellow-seekers after truth, and through fellowship with them in all possible ways, without sacrificing any deep Christian conviction, seek to lead them into a fuller acceptance of Him whom Christians in different ways believe to have been the complete revelation of God to man?

Index

INDEX

INDEX

Dead, offerings to, 182
Dead Sea Scrolls, 2
Death of Buddha, 44; of Confucius, 119; of Jesus, 44; of Krishna, 50; of Mahavira, 81; of Mohammed, 196; of Moses, 164, 183; of Nanak, 95; of Zoroaster, 153, 154
Deborah, 180
Decalogue, 171
Demons, 85
Desire, 28
Deuteronomy, 181
Deuteronomic Code, 168
Devaki, 47, 48, 50
Devananda, 75
Devas, 33
De Vita Mosis, 187
Devotion, 156
Dhamma, 35
Dinkhart, 147
Disciples, 30 176; of Buddha, 38; of Confucius, 119
Divecha, 158, 159
Divine Light, 218
Divorce, Moslem, 200; Christian, 200
Djinn, 219
Doctrine of human nature, Confucius, 123; of Jesus, 124
Doctrine of the decrees, 207
Doctrine of the Mean, 118, 122
Doctrine of the Perfect Man, 216
Documentary theory of the Hexateuch, 163
Dragon, 109, 132
Drinking, 29, 35
Dualism, 156
Dughdova, 149

Earthquake, 18
Ecclesia, 175
Egypt, 1, 164, 177, 185
Eight-fold path, 28, 29, 34, 83
Election, doctrine of, 81, 207; Sikh, 101
Elephant, 23; white, 18
Emmaus, 13
Enemies, 9; love of, 64, 78, 201
Enlightenment, 25, 35, 41, 43
Epigram, 119
Eros, 37
Escape birth, 80
Eschatology, Zoroastrian, 158-159
Essence of Mohammed, 216
Essenes, 2, 22, 189
Esther, 184
Ethical Basis of Buddhism, 38; of Christianity, 38

Ethical monotheism, 172
Ethics, of Confucius, 127; of Krishna, 58-59; of Lao-tzu, 141-143; of Mahavira, 80; of Mohammed, 212; of Moses, 181; of Nanak, 103; of Zoroaster, 154*ff.*
Evil, 38; destroyed, 159
Eye for an eye, 9, 36, 201
Ezra, 163

Faith, 160
Family, Confucius idea, 125
Fasting, 98
Fatherhood of God, 125
Female infanticide, 200
Filial piety, 125
First Sermon at Benares, 28
Five precepts, the, 35
Fleg, Edmund, 163, 169
Flight to Medina, 195
Fordfinders, 73, 77, 82
Forgiveness, 44, 83, 202
Four Noble Truths, 28
Free will, 157, 213
Freud, Sigmund, 167
Fundamentalists, 193
Future life, Confucius, 125; Jesus, 182; Krishna, 69-70; Mohammed, 213; Moses, 182; Zoroaster, 151

Gabars, 146
Gabriel, 185, 192, 197
Galilee, 4
Gandhi, M., 45, 61, 154
Gathas, 146, 152, 153, 154
Gautama, 23
General judgment, Zoroastrian, 152, 159
Gethsemane, Garden of, 11, 120, 176
Gita, the (*see* Bhagavad Gita), 51, 56
Gita Govinda, 49
Gobind Singh, 104, 105
God, 14, 73, 81, 91, 92; as Father, 38, 82, 181, 205, 206; as judge, 205, 208; as love, 206; as moral authoritiy, 212; Confucius' idea, 125-126; impersonal, 126; in Buddhism, 30; in *Gita,* 68; in popular Taoism, 138; Jesus' idea, 64, 125, 135, 181, 205; judgment of, 65; Krishna's idea, 64; Lao-tzu's idea, 136; man-god, 14; Mohammed's idea, 205; Moses' idea, 170, 171; Nanak's idea, 100; oneness of, 65; personal, 126, 205; Sikh idea, 96; unity of, 213; Zoroaster's idea, 151

INDEX

Gods, 30, 85
Golden Age, 130
Golden rule, Confucius, 123; Mahavira, 80
Goliath, 180
Good and evil, Zoroaster, 152
Good deeds, 157
Goodenough, E. R., 186, 188, 189
Good for evil, 204; Jesus, 143; Lao-tzu, 142
Good thought, 149, 150, 156
Good works, 93
Great Commission of Buddha, 33; of Jesus, 33
Gur Das, 104
Guru, 87, 95, 97; divine, 92; divinity of, 106
Guruship, doctrine of, 104; essence of, 105

Hadith, 193
Hagiographa, 184
Hamilton, C. H., 32, 33
Hasan, 219
Hate, 9
Hatred, 36
Haurvatat, 156
Heaven, 35, 44, 108, 131; as God, 125; Christian, 42; Jain, 84; Sikh, 102
Hebrew faith, 151
Hebrews, 44, 164, 204
Hegira, the, 195
Hell, Buddhist, 44; Jain, 84; Sikh, 102
Herod, 165
Hidden years, the, 2
Himalayas, 18, 21
Hinayana Buddhism, 40, 41, 42
Hinduism, 28, 37, 42, 46, 86, 90
Historical Records, The, 110, 114
Holiness Code, 168
Holy man, 25, 91, 98
Holy Sacrament, 45
Holy Trinity, 128
Homer, 147
Honesty, 35
Householder, 25, 35
House of Song, 152
House of the Lie, 152
Humility, in Jesus, 142; in Lao-tzu, 143
Husain, 219

Ikbal Ali Shah, 192, 218
Imam, 89
Imamate, 218
Imams, as intercessors, 219

Immortality, 156; Babylonian, 182; Confucius' idea, 125; Jesus' idea, 102; Moses' idea, 182; personal, 102; Zoroaster's idea, 151
Incarnation, 4, 60; Christian, 54; doctrine of, 53; Hindu, 53; multiple, 53; the tenth, 71-72
India, 2, 15
Indian Christ, 48
Individual, 70, 101, 152
Individuality, loss of, 102
Indra, 49
Intoxicants, 35
Isaiah, 171
Islam, 37, 90, 214; and brotherhood, 211
Israel, 167, 181

Jackson, A. V. W., 153
Jade Emperor, 144
Jaina Sutras, 78
Jainism, humanistic, 82
Jains, 26, 73, 75
Janam sakhi, 94
Japan, 41
Japji, 92, 96, 100
Jatakas, 17, 33
Jerusalem, 11
Jesus, 1-14, 20, 26, 27, 31, 42, 47, 74, 76, 80, 87, 97, 109, 118, 134, 150, 219; activist, 139, 141; a Jew, 212; and Buddha, 15-45, differences, 43*ff.*, likenesses, 36*ff.*; and Confucius, 108-131, differences, 118-120, 125-127, likenesses, 118*ff.*; and government, 154; and his mother, 8; and immortality, 68-69; and healing, 10; and killing, 78; and Krishna, 46-72, demand loyalty, 57, differences, 60*ff.*, incarnations, 53, likenesses, 52*ff.*, universal in outlook, 56; and Lao-tzu, 132-146, differences, 135*ff.*, likenesses, 134*ff.*; Mahavira, 73-85, differences, 81*ff.*, likenesses, 75*ff.*; and Mohammed, 191-220, differences, 196*ff.*, likenesses, 208*ff.*; and Moses, 161-190, differences, 173*ff.*, likenesses, 165*ff.*; and Nanak, 86-107, differences, 99*ff.*, likenesses, 89*ff.*; and sin, 45; and social problems, 211; and the church, 175; and the cult, 178, 212; and the state, 141; and violence, 202; and war, 37, 142, 154, 203; and Zoroaster, 146-160, differences, 153*ff.*, likenesses, 149; and Simeon, 21; and sinners, 7;

INDEX

INDEX

INDEX

Path of Light, The, 43
Paul, St., 13, 45, 80, 81, 136, 161, 179, 207, 214
Pavry, J.C.D., 160
Peace, 45
Pearl of great price, 5
Pentateuch, 162, 163, 177, 184
Pentecost, 13, 176
Perfect Man, doctrine of, 216
Persecution, of Jesus, 11; of Mohammed, 211
Persian, 90
Personal immortality, 44
Peter, St., 11, 177
Pharaoh, 165, 166
Pharisees, 8
Philip, 14
Philo, 188
Philosophy, Confucian, 129; Taoist, 134
Piety, 156
Pilgrimage, Moslem, 219; Sikh, 104
Pollock, Channing, 13
Polygamy, 199, 200
Polytheism, 138
Popular Islam, 219
Pourucista, 149
Pouruhaspa, 149
Pratt, J.B., 39, 40
Prayer, 31, 85, 129, 159; Jain, 84; of Jesus, 34, 209; of Mohammed, 209; of Santideva, 43; to Buddha, 42; to Confucius, 129; to Moses, 189; to Nanak, 106
Predestination, 217
Prodigal Son, 7
Promised Land, 168, 185
Prophet, The, 193, 202, 214, 219; sinlessness of, 215
Prophethood, doctrine of, 215; of Mohammed, 215
Prophets, 162, 172, 184
Propitiation, 129
Propriety, 116
Protestant, 175
Proverbs, 168
Providence, 191
Psalms, 168, 180, 181
Pure Land, 42
Puri, 94
Purity, 35
Purna, 36

Rabbinical writings, 163
Rabbis, the 189
Radha, 49
Radhakrishnan, S., 46
Rama, 54, 100

Ram Das, 105
Rayapur, 89
Reality, 31
Rebek, 92
Rebirth, 30, 32, 73, 101
Redemption, 38, 44
Red Sea, 167
Release, 38
Religion, 93
Religions of the Book, 194
Remission of sins, 45, 157
Renunciation of Buddha, 45
Repentance, 38, 45
Retribution, 38, 212
Revival, Jain, 79, 85
Right action, 29
Right aims, 29
Right contemplation, 29
Right effort, 29
Righteousness, 43, 58, 59, 154, 157
Right living, 29
Right mindfulness, 29
Right speech, 29
Right views, 29
Rishabhadeva, 73
Roman Catholic Church, 175
Romans, 9
Rome, 11

Sach Khand, 102
Sacred Literature, 16
Sacrifice, 14
Sadhus, 90
Sage, The, 129, 131
Saint Paul, 190 (*see* Paul)
Sakyamuni, 42
Salvation, 14, 55, 59, 69, 70, 81, 101, 103; Buddhist, 30, 40; by faith, Sikh, 97, Buddhist, 38, 42, 52; cat way, 70; Christian, 31; Hindu, 52, 55; in history, 139; Jain, 73, 83; Lao-tzu, 138-139; monkey way, 71; Moslem, 207; Sikh, 97, 99; universal, in Jainism, 88; in Jesus' teaching, 81; Zoroaster, 157, 160
Samadhi, 32
Sangha, the, 35, 39
Santideva, 43
Saoshyant, savior, 159
Satan, 3, 27, 93, 156
Savior, in Buddhism, 42-43; in Christianity, 14; in Hinduism, 55; in Judaism, 186; in Sikhism, 104; in Zoroastrianism, 159
Scriptures, Buddhist, 16; Sikh, 87
Second Coming, 71
Second Isaiah, 171

INDEX

INDEX

Vardhamana, 76
Vasudaeva, 47, 50, 75
Vedas, 75
Vendidad, 160
Veneration of Saints, 219
Vicarious suffering, 126
Violence, Krishna and, 61; Moham-
 med and, 201*ff*.; Zoroaster, 154
Virgin birth, 20, 159
Vishnu, 47, 50, 52, 53, 54, 89
Vishnu, the Preserver, 66
Vishnu Purana, 58
Vishtaspa, 154
Vohu Mano, 149, 156
Voice of Ahimsa, 79

Wahabis, 219
Waley, Arthur, 114, 116, 133
War, 45; Arjuna's protest, 61-62;
 Buddha and, 37; Confucius and,
 127; Jesus and, 37, 142; Lao-tzu
 and, 142; Mohammed and, 203;
 Moses and, 180; Zoroaster and,
 154*ff*.
Western Paradise, 42
Wheel, the, 81, 101
Wild Union, 110
Wing-tsit Chan, 109
Wisdom of Confucius, 115
Wisdom of Lao-tzu, 133
Women, Attitude of Buddha, 39; of
 Mohammed, 199-200
Woodward, F.L., 30
Work of Christ, 14
Works, 160
World-soul, 66

World view of Jesus, 81*ff*.
World War, 37
Worship in the early church, 174;
 Jain, 82
Wu wei, 140; and government, 140

Yahweh, 164, 171; and war, 180;
 jealous, 180; storm god, 179*ff*.
Yasodha, 48
Yogi, 93
Yogin, 29

Zaid, 192
Zaratusht Namah, 147, 148
Zoroaster and Jesus, 146-160, differences, 153*ff*., likenesses, 150*ff*.;
 and government, 154; and Sermon
 on the Mount, 155; and war, 154-
 155; annunciation of, 148; as
 judge, 159; birth of, 148; call of,
 150; childhood of, 148, 149; date
 of, 146, 147; death of, 153-154;
 facts concerning, 149, 150; future
 life idea, 182; key to salvation,
 158; leaves home, 149; legends of,
 149; marriage, 153; method of
 work, 154; miracles of, 149, 158;
 prophet, 157; reformer, 157; seed
 of, 159; sense of mission of, 150;
 sources for, 146*ff*.; tempted, 150;
 thought concerning, 157*ff*.; wanderings of, 150; was he deified?
 159
Zoroastrianism, influence on Christianity, 152
Zoroastrian Sacred Literature, 146